Hope and Justice for All in the Americas

Discerning God's Mission

Edited by Oscar L. Bolioli

Friendship Press • New York

Editorial Offices:
475 Riverside Drive, New York, NY 10115

Distribution Offices:
PO Box 37844, Cincinnati, OH 45222-0844

Unless otherwise indicated, Scripture quotations are from the New Revised Standard Version of the Bible, copyright 1989 by the Division of Christian Education of the National Council of the Churches of Christ in the USA. Used by permission. All rights reserved.

Manufactured in the United States of America

Library of Congress Cataloging-in-Publication Data

Hope and justice for all in the Americas : discerning God's mission
/ Oscar L. Bolioli, editor.
    p.   cm.
    Essays presented at a missiology consultation in San Jose, Costa Rica,
    Apr. 21-25, 1997.
    Includes bibliographical references.
    ISBN 0-377-00325-5
    1. Missions—Latin America—Theory—Congresses. 2. Sociology,
    Christian—Latin America—Congresses. 3. Missions, American—Latin
    America—Congresses. 4. Sociology, Christian—United States—
    Congresses. 5. National Council of the Churches of Christ in the
    United States of America—Congresses. I. Bolioli, Oscar L.
    BV2831.H65 1998
    266'.0098—dc21

Because of the tight production schedule for this book, there was no time to research incomplete end notes.

Cover design: Paul Lansdale
Book design and layout: Nanako Inoue
Cover photo: NACLA Report on the Americas, copyright 1998 by
    The North American Congress on Latin America

Table of Contents

continued on next page

Foreword

The Missiology Consultation in San José, Costa Rica, April 21-25, 1997, was a landmark event that brought church leaders from Latin America, Central America, and the Caribbean together with leaders from ten mission agencies from the United States. It was the first such event since the Havana Conference in 1929. And it was a very different occasion. Almost seventy years later, the churches are struggling with a variety of new issues: effects of economic globalization, degradation of the environment, fragmentation of the family, and a host of other matters that were not part of earlier agendas. Furthermore, today the churches are confronted with an important new challenge as the burgeoning Pentecostal movement, in all its richness and complexity, demands the attention of churches that previously dismissed it.

There have been many mission conferences since the historic gathering in Edinburgh, Scotland, in 1910, that is often called the birthplace of the ecumenical movement. The San José conference, like the one in Edinburgh, sought to reflect critically on the mission of the church in its own day. In San José, we of the church were called to witness in our own particular socioeconomic context, even as some of the problems that beset us wreak havoc with our societies, both in the North and the South.

But we are not a people without hope or vision. Our hope is God's shalom, which comes to us in life, in ministry, and in the resurrection of Jesus. Harvey Cox, theologian and author, said it memorably in his conference presentation: "Throughout the gospels, Jesus manifests the coming of God's shalom in both verbal and enacted parables, in deeds of mercy and healing, and in stern warnings to those who sinfully misuse power and privilege to deter the full realization of God's reign. After his death at the hands of those who represent the political, economic, and religio-cultural opposition to the coming of this reign, God raised Jesus from the dead as a vindication of his mission and sent the Holy Spirit to empower men and women of faith to continue it." In a sea of poverty and powerlessness, the church in Latin America remains an island of hope in the way it responds to the signs of the times and a place where the gospel is being rediscovered and renewed with fresh power.

i

The San José mission consultation could not have succeeded without the participation and support of many individuals and organizations. We wish to express our deep and abiding gratitude to all who made presentations or contributed financially. The planning committee, under the direction of the Reverend Oscar L. Bolioli, did a superb job of working out the myriad details of the conference. The Bible studies, led by Dr. Elsa Tamez, were deeply enriching. Dr. John H. Sinclair's presentation, with its synopsis of mission in Latin America since the 1916 Panama Congress, was invaluable in establishing the historical context of the San José event. The inspiring worship services were bound together by the singing of beautiful and appropriate hymns led by a group of talented musicians from the Pentecostal church in Maracaibo, Venezuela.

We spent almost a week of intensive work: worshiping together, singing together, studying the Bible together, and listening to what God is telling us today, seeking to be God's agents of justice, compassion, and reconciliation, praying that the reign of God may become a reality among us.

Rodney I. Page, Executive Director
Church World Service and Mission
National Council of the Churches of Christ in the USA.

And a Word of Thanks

Translators of Spanish- and Portuguese-language essays: ■ **Joyce Hill** served as a missionary of the United Methodist Church in Cuba, Argentina, and Chile. She has translated works from Spanish and Portuguese for the Methodists and the National Council of Churches. ■ **Donald Reasoner** is a minister of the United Methodist Church on special assignment to the Latin American and Caribbean region. He works primarily on short-term projects with UMC churches and agencies ■ **Mariela Shaw** is program specialist in the Latin America and the Caribbean Office of the National Council of Churches. Her translations have appeared in a wide range of publications.

Photographer: ■ **Ana Aslan**, a freelance photographer, recently won the AT&T Artsline Award and first mention in the Latin American photographic essay award in Havana, Cuba. She has worked for Church World Service in Mexico and Ethiopia.

Introduction

In 1910 representatives of U.S. mission societies left the Edinburgh World Missionary Conference deeply troubled by agreements adopted by European mission societies, declaring Latin America a continent already "Christianized." The Conference on Mission Work in Latin America, held in New York in 1913, voiced those concerns and restated its confidence in the work of the Committee on Cooperation with Latin America (CCLA). This is the heritage that undergirds, to this day, the work of the Committee on Latin America and the Caribbean of the National Council of the Churches of Christ in the USA.

In 1916 Panama was host to the Congress on Christian Work in Latin America. The congress met again in Montevideo in 1925, and, once more, in Havana in 1929. Three further consultations—each known as the Latin American Evangelical Conference—were held between 1949 and 1969, concentrating on issues of the South.

In 1986 the Committee on the Caribbean and Latin America (successor to the Committee on Cooperation with Latin America), began the São Paulo Process, an arrangement that sought to change the ways in which sister churches and institutions in Latin America and the Caribbean worked with one another and with mission boards in the North. The underlying concept was to concentrate on developing a collegial, "shared" way of working together. As Bishop Rafael Malpica-Padilla expressed it during the consultation in Costa Rica, the São Paulo Process "overcomes the church donor-church recipient dichotomy to open a new way of understanding and doing mission."

In 1991 conversations expanded by including the Caribbean Conference of Churches and the Latin American Council of Churches about the need for a process to study and establish dialogue between mission boards in the United States and churches in Latin America and the Caribbean. It was agreed that the U.S. mission boards needed to confer with one another in order to define their role, and that this might lead to a larger and more inclusive consultation in the future.

CCLA began a conversation with the ten largest U.S. mission boards that work in Latin America and the Caribbean and are members of the National Council of the Churches of Christ in the USA. This dialogue was expanded to include representatives from programs and projects in the region, culminating in the Missiology Consultation held in San José, Costa Rica, on April 21-25, 1997. Participants included delegates from churches in the South and from ten U.S. mission boards; representatives of peasants, indigenous peoples, women, and youth; representatives of regional and worldwide councils of churches; and the fraternal presence of Roman Catholic and other nonconciliar delegates. For five days, 118 persons engaged in prayer, study, celebration, and the search for ways of doing mission together in imaginative ways that address the hopes and needs of all God's people.

Much of what we have achieved is because of the contributions and the knowledge of Michael Rivas, Bill Nottingham, Zwinglio Dias, and Elsa Tamez. Offered, herewith, are the presentations and conclusions of this consultation and a number of earlier mini-consultations, with the hope that they will help those of us who are the church to continue and deepen the dialogue with our Southern and Northern sisters and brothers in Christ.

Oscar L. Bolioli, Director
Latin America and the Caribbean Office
Church World Service and Witness
National Council of the Churches of Christ in the USA

Message to Our Churches and Communities

From Participants in the Missiology Consultation

As drafted by the consultation writing team:
Oscar L. Bolioli, David Bronkema,
Anastasio Gallego,Rafael Malpica-Padilla,
David A. Vargas.

"To you then who believe, he is precious;
but for those who do not believe, 'The stone that
the builders rejected has become the
very head of the corner.'" (1 Peter 2:7)

Called together for a Missiology Consultation in San José, Costa Rica, sponsored by the National Council of the Churches of Christ in the USA (NCCCUSA) from April 21-25, 1997, to reflect about mission, representatives of mission boards in the United States—African Methodist Episcopal Church, African Methodist Episcopal Zion Church, American Baptist Churches, Church of the Brethren, Christian Church (Disciples of Christ), United Church of Christ, Episcopal Church, Evangelical Lutheran Church in America, Presbyterian Church (USA), Reformed Church in America, United Methodist Church—met with brothers and sisters from churches in Latin America and the Caribbean invited by their partners in the United States; and with representatives from the World Council of Churches (WCC), the Latin American Council of Churches (CLAI), the Caribbean Conference of Churches (CCC), and the United Church of Canada, as well as from institutions and ecumenical programs related to the NCCCUSA through their participation in the São Paulo Process.

We arrived in San José to reflect on a process of coordination and a better understanding of mission in Latin America and the Caribbean among mission boards in the United States. That process began at Panama in 1916 and continued with the 1925 Montevideo and 1929 Havana congresses. It now takes on new meaning, spurred by questions about the significance of mission today, and has provided new content to our relationship between churches in the North and the South. If Panama was witness to a monologue by mis-

1

sion boards in the United States, in San José there was an effort to create dialogue by expanding the circle of interlocutors. As a consequence of this dialogue, we feel called upon as the church to ask forgiveness of the original peoples of these continents and of other excluded sectors, because we are, in part, responsible for the silence and for the complicity with the powers of the world. If in Panama, Latin America and the Caribbean were seen as objects of mission, in San José we helped one another recognize ourselves as co-participants in God's mission.

As we prayed, reflected together, exchanged experiences of mission, and sought for mutual cooperation between brothers and sisters from the South and the North, these five days enabled us to discern some challenges faced by the churches today. It was the result of a search for mutual cooperation between brothers and sisters from the continent's North and South.

Our reflection, which we want to share with our churches and communities, had four central themes:

- hunger for bread, hunger for God, and hunger for humanity
- the gospel and culture
- ecumenism today
- mission as a responsibility of all

As we shared experiences and received information, it became clear that the present time is dominated by the omnipresence of the market system—an idol that demands exclusion of the weakest, who have been transformed into migrants, prostitutes, and street children as a result of unemployment, poverty, and racial and gender discrimination. These, the excluded, the victims of the system, become "the stones rejected by the builders" of the society of the new millennium, in the North as well as the South. The presence of those in our society who are excluded from the goods of the Creator confronts the church with questions of its faithfulness to the gospel's justice in the face of unjust economic systems.

We are aware that the dominant cultures in the North have established the current forms of proclaiming the gospel, presenting it and their culture as the determinate way of life. The irruption of indigenous peoples, peoples of African descent, and women, forgotten or made invisible in the past, poses a challenge to white religious and cultural hegemony. The plurality of cultures and religious expressions today goes beyond the denominational variety. The presence of many diverse indigenous, African American, and Eastern religions, among others, makes Latin America and the Caribbean a religiously pluralistic region. This fact challenges Christian churches to approach ecumenism with a change in mind and spirit that will lead us to new structures at the service of a new *oikumene,* generating and strengthening hope in the God of life.

In the study of the Scriptures, we saw Job on the garbage heap, demanding an explanation for injustice; Paul telling the Galatians that they were called to be sons and daughters of God, and not slaves; and Peter asking us to be living stones, because those that were rejected by the builder were chosen by God.

The strength of the Word moves us to make and call others to assume commitments that we understand to be urgent:

- We affirm dialogue with and respect for different cultures; that the gospel become incarnate in each culture; and that each culture has the right to live the gospel and express it in its own way. We recognize that we have been responsible in part for the exclusion of those from other cultures, and their way of expressing faith, either through our silence or in our practices. We must deepen in our churches reflection about culture and gospel and lead the church to become transformed into a space for encounter and reconciliation.

- We affirm that the time of the missionary from the North, ready to "civilize" and to inculcate Northern culture, has passed. It is time for a common mission of all, because witness and commitment go beyond denominational borders. A common mission is framed in new initiatives with and in solidarity with the socially and economically excluded; it is a common mission to engage in the prophetic denunciation of systems that exclude. In the defense of life and creation, and in the struggle against corruption and impunity are created the signs of the reign that is already present but is yet to come.

- We affirm the call of the Jubilee in the year 2000 to benefit the poorest, leading to forgiveness of the debt that overwhelms countries in the South and each year sacrifices thousands of lives; a Jubilee that will break the master and slave relationship and restore us to being brothers and sisters full of humanity in a world and a church with room for all.

- We are witnesses to the action of the Holy Spirit in a new Pentecost that is sweeping the hemisphere, North and South, awakening, dislodging, removing structures, questioning tranquillities and securities, opening new spaces, and bringing hope.

- We call on everyone, especially the mission boards in the United States, to join forces in concrete effort against signs of egoism and perversity that work against mission—such as, for example, the lifting of regulations prohibiting the sale of sophisticated arms to the South—because such actions divert resources that should be used to alleviate serious human and social problems. The new migration law in the United States—another example—is exclusionary, xenophobic, and utilitarian. The embargo against other nations, especially Cuba, is a sign of intolerance because, again, it victimizes innocent persons.

Those of us who have participated in this consultation commit ourselves to share our gifts and talents, to continue the dialogue that has been initiated, and to celebrate our work together, proclaiming that "the Spirit of the Lord is upon me, because he has anointed me to bring good news to the poor. He has sent me to proclaim release to the captives and recovery of sight to the blind, to let the oppressed go free, to proclaim the year of the Lord's favor" (Luke 4:18-19).

Mission Within the Framework of the São Paulo Process: Achievements and Aspirations

Compiled by Zwinglio M. Dias

Zwinglio M. Dias received his doctorate in theology
from the University of Hamburg, Germany.
He is a Presbyterian pastor in a favela in Rio de Janeiro,
and a member of the *Koinonia* team

This essay is a summary of the conclusions reached by participants in the regional mini-consultations that preceded the 1997 Missiology Consultation held in Costa Rica, April 1997, and sponsored by the National Council of the Churches of Christ in the USA.

Unfortunately, as often happens, the final documents of those meetings do not reflect the richness of the discussions. At times such documents can be almost telegraphic, consigning important themes to a few brief phrases that merit deeper discussion. We found it necessary to read between the lines, struggling to be faithful to the content, and to resist the temptation to interpret, which would have been dishonest and arrogant.

The Context of Mission

The reports do not concern themselves with extensive descriptions of the general context of Latin America and the Caribbean; rather, they are clear, concise observations that reflect the participants' understanding of the reality within which their activities are carried out. Here, in summary form, are some of them:

- The lives of the people who have been touched by the missionary effort are lived out in a "context of poverty" and "savage capitalism" that proclaims and secures "globalization at the service of increasingly fewer people, converting the eagerness for profit, money, and capital into a god who demands sacrifices without concern for the social and human cost that must be paid."

- "[Like] all empires in the history of humanity, the preponderance of force, militarism, state terrorism, and impunity traps our peoples in a systematic violation of their rights, challenging all those who seek justice and peace." Today, then, life occurs in "situations of death, not only physical, but also spiritual."

- "Our people face harsh adjustments in their daily lives as a result of unemployment, hunger, school desertion, prostitution, transculturation, repression, frustration, and deception—in short, despair, agony, and death."

Traditional Missionary Paradigms

Participants in the mini-consultations did not spend much time reflecting on traditional missionary paradigms. It became clear early in the discussions that traditional missionary programs—tilted toward reproducing ecclesiastical structures—no longer respond to the demands of the situation lived by people in Latin America and the Caribbean. The groups had information about the purposes and scope of the planned 1997 missiology consultation and they learned about the significance of the 1916 Panama Congress as a frame of reference for the missionary work of Protestant churches since then.

At the same time, the regional groups recognized that the style of Protestantism–North American in origin—refashioned and consolidated through revival movements of the eighteenth and nineteenth centuries is relevant to the modernizing process of Latin American and Caribbean societies because it is "the type of Protestantism linked to the liberal ideas of the era, behind the idea of separation of Church and State that promoted education of lay persons, social work, the service of an integrated gospel." Nevertheless, the groups pointed out, not only mission boards in the United States, but also the churches that are the result of mission, are called to rethink traditional approaches and to formulate proposals in response to challenges imposed by today's societies that seek new ways of doing mission. This is true not only in a socioeconomic context, but also because of the emergence of new, faith-based structures that are not consolidated expressions of "historical" Protestantism, as well as the emergence of new social protagonists and alternative practices that challenge the missionary work of Christians on the continent.

A New and Developing Model for Mission

Analyzing their practices in the context of their subregions, in the light of their understanding of the gospel, and with the background of traditional missionary practices, the groups attempted to express a new perspective for the missionary activity of Christian communities, affirming mission in the following ways:
- *Defending life* by defending human rights in civil, political, social, cultural, and ecological ways

- *Building awareness and providing education and training* for people about their condition and values and the possibilities for emerging with faith and hope from misery and despair
- *Offering a radical option for life*, affirming the possibility of a full life in both the material and spiritual sense, including experiences of esthetic enjoyment, development of creativity, and affirmation of the dignity of every human being
- *Affirming an ethical and political imperative* that understands salvation to be the building of solidarity with those who live in situations of death
- *Accepting diversity and dialogue* within a pluralistic society
- *Maintaining solidarity* as the *sine qua non* of authentic missionary experience, especially with those victimized by socioeconomic structures
- *Developing the creative gifts of God's people* in any and all circumstances
- *Being open without reservation* to the activity of God's Spirit in the world
- *Being prophetic,* actively denouncing the injustice of socioeconomic structures and of imposed Christianity; disdain of the cultural diversity of the region's peoples; and ignorance about and condemnation of the religious expressions of indigenous and African-Latin American peoples
- *Actively redeeming the humanity of Latin American and Caribbean women,* who are subjugated and discriminated against, presenting a human face of absolute poverty–spiritual as well as material
- *Recreating spirituality* in people that they may respond with integrity and honesty to religious questions and needs
- *Defining new identities* exploring who we are and who others are; witnessing to what we are and what we believe; and creating ecumenical communities that reflect the diversity and plurality of our peoples

Priorities and Challenges for Mission Today

Starting with their own experiences and visions, the regional groups drew up the following list of priorities and challenges to Christian action that would make such action more relevant to people seeking to follow Jesus in their particular Latin American contexts:

Priorities

- *Seeking integrated efforts* to be carried out in each region and to produce significant strategic linkages among them
- *Consolidating actions of solidarity* in crisis situations in order to respond efficiently to conjunctural or ongoing needs as expressions of the interdependence that defines us as Christians
- *Rethinking ecumenism* in terms of integration and unity for mission, starting from the base of our organizations and churches. This redefinition, when exposed to people's amplification, will result in a common—and significant—experience.
- *Developing a community reference point* for carrying out mission and providing feedback for our work. There is a need to recognize small and incremental changes in the struggle against poverty.
- *Conceiving integrated responses* to felt needs, avoiding the old and nonfunctional dichotomy between mission and service
- *Understanding mission* as directed not only toward the outside, but also inside, amongst ourselves, in the sense of becoming open to the experiences of other religions
- *Understanding mission* as the product of a diaconal witness community far removed from proselytizing attitudes

Challenges

- *Change in language.* Missiological activity demands a change of language in the framework of a new concept of life and practice.
- *Search for a new ethic.* Together, we must overcome the concepts and practices that have been in place until the present day, so that we may construct a new ethic for life based on recognizing our own identity and that of the other; on developing a growing self-esteem; and on constructing a spirit of solidarity, justice, work, love, and pleasure.
- *Cultural activity.* Mission should be understood as a cultural activity because it is not determined by a cost-benefit relationship. It is closely aligned with the creation of values—a cultural enterprise.
- *Prophetic activity.* Mission in the face of limiting situations is always prophetic because it seeks to construct values that challenge or are in conflict with the system.
- *The valuing of corporeality.* This new category makes possible thought and action concerning issues of gender by creating new

forms of alternative social relationships that occur within frame-works of power and discrimination.

- *Rejection of idolatry.* Idolatry will be rejected by recovering the prophetic force of Christianity with its affirmation of faith in the God of life.
- *Increase in North-South dialogue.* Dialogue is necessary for building solidarity between regions, enhancing the horizon of hope in a new world.

Ecumenism:
An Evolving Vision of
Mission, Unity, and Service

Joan Brown Campbell

Joan Brown Campbell, a minister in the Christian
Church (Disciples of Christ) and American Baptist
Churches in the USA, is general secretary of the National
Council of the Churches of Christ in the USA.

I am honored to address this historic gathering and to support the
continuation of three consultations that have been of great significance to mission in my nation and Canada, Latin America, and the
Caribbean. We come together at a crucial time to seek new ways of
cooperation, to fashion new models for doing mission, perhaps to
reenergize old, familiar ways. To be in this part of the world, discussing this subject, is especially poignant for me, personally. Thirty
years ago, as an active member of a congregation in Cleveland,
Ohio, I went on what was to be the first of many ecumenical learning journeys. I was privileged to visit Latin America under the tute-
lage of T.J. Liggett and William Nottingham, both past presidents of
the Division of Overseas Ministries of the Christian Church
(Disciples of Christ); both pioneers of ecumenism.

It was, as I recall, a journey focused on mission and unity. These
two men knew well a lesson that I fear is being lost; that mission and
unity cannot be separated. The suffering of God's people demands a
response—a full, prayerful, sacrificial response. Neither the brand
name of a denomination nor that of a nation-state dares be the measure of that response, as official documents of the World Council of
Churches have put it. That early trip introduced me to liberation theology. The concern for the visible unity of Christ's church may never
be considered apart from concern for Christian proclamation, witness, and service in a world crying out for renewal. To separate these
two themes is to forget that Jesus' prayer for unity was for the sake of
the world. But, despite our hesitation, the freeing, liberating hand of
God moves in our time, and events press us to a more whole and a
more complete understanding of unity—more inclusive of religion,
race, gender, and nationality.

The Ecumenical Education of God's People

Perhaps one of the major ecumenical challenges facing us in the 1990s is the ecumenical education of God's people. There is a serious temptation in our time to leave ecumenism to the professionals—denominational staff people and those institutions we have created to be our ecumenical voice (the Consultation on Church Union, local councils of churches, the National Council of Churches, the World Council of Churches, the Council of Churches in Latin America). Of course, support of these visible agents is an urgent matter, but equally important is the "ecumenizing" of the people of God. One of the reasons we have so much controversy over our ecumenical institutions is because we have failed to create a climate for understanding their work and witness. Perhaps we have been reluctant to create this climate with the full understanding that a call for the reunion of creation and of all God's children is a very radical action. The quest for Christian unity is a response to the gospel of Jesus Christ: it is a recognition that God is on the side of all that unites, integrates, heals, and makes whole. It calls us to live beyond our human divisions.

A careful study of the Hebrew Bible and the New Testament reveals that the unity of the church and the unity of humankind are major themes in the Word of God. From the very beginning this is made clear. In the creation story there is an integrity and a wholeness in all that God creates; there is a purposeful interdependence between earth and people. All were meant to live in harmony with one another and with creation. This is beautifully expressed in a prayer of the Dakota nation:

> Grandfather, Great Spirit, you have always been and before you nothing has been. There is no one to pray to but you. The star nations all over the heavens are yours, and the grasses of the earth. You are older than all need, older than all pain and prayer. Grandfather, Grandmother, Great Spirit, all over the world the faces of the living ones are alike. With tenderness they have come up out of the ground. Look upon your children with children in their arms that they may face the winds and walk the good road until the day of quiet. Grandfather, Great Spirit, fill with the light, give us the strength to understand and eyes to see, teach us to walk the soft earth as relatives to all that are alive. Help us, for without you we are nothing.

The prophet Isaiah describes a world made whole when he offers the age-old word of hope to the people of Israel:

> For I am about to create new heavens and a new earth; the former things shall not be remembered or come to mind. . . . No more shall the sound of weeping be heard in it, or the cry of distress. No more shall there be in it an infant that lives but a few days. . . . They shall build houses and inhabit them; they shall plant vineyards and eat their fruit. They shall not build and another inhabit; they shall not plant and another eat. . . . They shall not labor in vain or bear children for calamity. . . . They shall not hurt or destroy on all my holy mountain, says the Lord" (Isaiah 65:17-25).

A Vision of God's Future

Isaiah's words are a vision of God's future, a reuniting of God's people with God and with one another, a future where the tree of peace, whose roots are justice, will flourish. The same theme is found in Micah 4:3-4, where peace and economic justice are joined into one. The New Testament is rich in ecumenical imagery also. Over and over, the theme of unity is reinforced: "With all wisdom and insight he has made known to us the mystery of his will, according to his good pleasure that he set forth in Christ, as a plan for the fullness of time, to gather up all things in him, things in heaven and things on earth" (Ephesians 1:8-9). The same thought is repeated in Colossians, and in John it is simply: "So there will be one flock, one shepherd" (John 10:16). In Galatians the unity of humankind is set forth: "There is no longer Jew or Greek . . . there is no longer male and female, for all of you are one in Christ Jesus" (Galatians 3:28). In Ephesians we are begged to live in recognition of the reality that "There is one body and . . . one Spirit . . . one Lord, one faith, one baptism" (Ephesians 4:4-5).

If we ever wonder why the church works diligently to remove all barriers of race, sex, class, denomination, nation-state, handicapping condition, or sexual preference that separate the people of God from one another, we need only to read again Ephesians 2:11-19. Here, those set against each other are made one and God creates a new humanity where none are strangers or sojourners but all are fellow citizens among the saints and members of the household of God. If one reads the Scriptures carefully, one can only draw the conclusion that the church must be the sign and foretaste of the unity within which God calls God's people to live, not so that the church might succeed but "that they may all be one . . . so that the world may believe" (cf. John 17:21).

Faith itself is ecumenical. Dietrich Bonhoeffer, who gave his life for what he believed, put it very clearly: "The raison d'etre for the ecumenical movement is not to save the church but to save human kind." Understanding the basics of the unity we seek helps us to envision the nature of our unity. The history of the ecumenical movement reveals clearly how our vision has expanded. If one were to look first at a picture of a meeting of the founders of the World Council of Churches, and then at a picture of a recent meeting of the World Council's Central Committee, the first picture would show Protestants, mostly Westerners of pale hue. The second picture would be very different, with images of Protestants and Orthodox Christians from all over the world, representing men and women of all races and a vast array of cultures. Those in the first picture were like-minded individuals who wrestled with questions of faith and order and service to those in need. Some would say it was a time of great leaders whose articulate voices still speak to us today. Indeed, they were great leaders. But that which constituted leadership was something commonly accepted and rarely debated. In many ways, these early days of the ecumenical movement were characterized by people who thought alike, seeking a difficult but commonly under-stood goal. Yet God had more in mind for the ecumenical move-ment. It was not to be a victory easily won. Because once you begin the process of inclusion, there is no ready peace in the house!

Unity of the Church and of Humankind

Until 1960 our quest for unity was, for the most part, focused on the church as institution. Here in the United States up to that time, we put our energies into seeking the organic unity of the churches. However, the turbulence of the '60s and the legitimate cries for lib-eration—especially in Latin America—and meaningful participation challenged the fullness of our ecumenical understanding. The Third World gained influence in the World Council of Churches. The Orthodox churches, including the Russian Orthodox Church, joined in large numbers. In the United States, the black churches began to make their voices heard in the Consultation on Church Union and in the National Council of Churches. And women stepped out the kitchen and the offices of religious education into the pulpit. Thus we were forcibly, passionately, brought face to face with the completeness and fullness of the meaning of the word "unity." One of the charismatic founders of the Christian Church (Disciples of Christ), Racoon John Smith, tried to tell us that when he said, "God has put but one people on the earth and He exhorts them to be one family."

As the World Council of Churches began to speak of the unity of the church and the unity of of humankind, a new and more whole understanding of unity began to be understood and articulated. It is this dream of unity that will carry us into the twenty-first century. This understanding of unity deals seriously with church union, but, if we are serious about words, it demands a further union—a sharing of power that recognizes past and present injustices. We can speak of unity as central to our faith, but it will never carry the day unless we realize that ending racism, sexism, and economic superiority and exploitation are part and parcel of that search for unity.

The struggle for justice and righteousness is not a struggle of our making. It is a gospel mandate. It is a struggle for an order of things that is surer than tomorrow's sunrise. I firmly believe that if we had truly internalized this truth, there would have been far fewer questions about the World Council of Churches' Programme to Combat Racism. It would have been understood as logical programmatic response to our commitment to be one people—a top priority for the ecumenical movement not because someone in Geneva or New York decreed it to be so, but because Jesus Christ is our Lord. The more we stress diversity and plurality, the more faithful and more difficult becomes our ecumenical task. The more clearly our world struggles against the forces of death, the more essential ecumenical action becomes.

The challenges facing denominations in the 1990s and beyond is to educate the people to be ecumenically minded. Then, and only then, will our churches be able to engage creatively in common mission and credible witness.

Our global interdependence invites an ecumenical response. Ways of ecumenical thinking and working are only beginning to emerge and take shape. Developing them is essential work for strengthening the foundations of what Dr. Martin Luther King, Jr. called "our world house." "We have inherited a large house," King wrote in one of his last essays, "a great world house in which we have to live together, Black and white, male and female, Jew and Gentile, Catholic and Protestant, Muslim and Hindu . . . . [We are] a family unduly separated in ideas, culture and interests who, because we can never again live apart, must somehow learn to live with each other in peace."

Where Are We in Our Quest?

Having stated the biblical mandate and the societal needs for unity, and having described the nature of the unity we seek, let us take a look at where we are in our quest. Our present ecumenical reality is a precarious one. I think any honest assessment must be confessional, for we have, in the main, been apathetic and passionless in our support of the ecumenical venture.

I am very much afraid that our mission ventures are characterized more by competition than by cooperation and that the need for credit for one's work, especially in a media-driven society, threatens carefully developed partnerships.

Denominational staff persons and those in positions of ecumenical leadership are experiencing frayed relationships. We come perilously close to blaming one another when, in fact, the insecurity—even chaos—we experience ought to drive us into one another's outstretched arms. And it is no easier today to be on the staff of a large white American denomination than it is be an ecumenical staff person. But, my friends, the Lord of history calls and we will be one people. As we come to the fiftieth anniversary of the World Council of Churches and the National Council of Churches, instruments born out of human vision, work, and witness, we need to craft for ourselves an ecumenical ship that will command our loyalty and carry our dreams. Our people are ready. Imagine for a few minutes what might happen in this conference if those attending were pastors and laity from our congregations—persons without a denomination's honor to protect or an ecumenical body's history to defend. They might make bold promises that we would have to carry out. Let them speak through our works. Until our commitment to unity is strengthened, our mission effectiveness will be limited.

Ecumenism is not primarily an institution to be preserved. It might be in my self-interest to tell you that preserving the National Council of Churches is absolutely essential as we move into the next century. But that is not what I want to say to you. Ecumenists are interfaith advocates, not those people who get paid professionally to make the ecumenical movement work. Ecumenism at its core is a way of seeing reality. It is a way of being. It is a methodology for doing. It is radical and life-changing. If loving my neighbor is a moral mandate, then my time is not my time alone. My money is not mine to hoard. My money is God-given. My talents are to be shared. I am to share in full generous measure what was shared with me. It is a radical understanding of life. My world cannot be small, confined, filled only with people who look and think as I do. We need, as the scientists say, the rich diversity of our planet. We need one another—desperately. Going it alone—again, as scientists say—is, finally, death-dealing. Life is found when everything relates to everything. We dare not tire of the ecumenical pilgrimage. We dare not get bored with it or cynical. For it is God's gift and challenge to us . It is sound science and good—very good—religion.

From Panama to San José: Eighty Years on an Ecumenical Journey

John H. Sinclair

John H. Sinclair, a graduate of Princeton
Theological Seminary, served as a missionary to
Venezuela and Chile, and as regional secretary for
Latin America for the mission board of the
Presbyterian Church (USA).

There are places and faces along the journey from Panama to San José: Panama, Montevideo, Buenos Aires, Havana, and Lima; faces of early missionaries from Great Britain and the United States; people such as Thomson and Taylor, Rembao and Rycroft, Martinez and Mackay, Braga and Browning, Ortz Gonzalez and Baez Camargo. This collage of places and people reveals a fascinating interplay of spiritual and historical forces that converged in Latin America over the past eighty years as evangelical Christianity moved into the spiritual vacuum of this region. We are the inheritors of that rich and complex history as we gather on Costa Rican soil today, both to look back and to envision the saga that lies before us in the next millennium.

Can we profit from this history of Christians struggling together across the twentieth century to respond together to Christ's call to mission in Latin America? Ruben Alves asks us to consider now at the close of the eighty years whether Protestantism has aged prematurely or lost much of its new insights and initial vision.

In his monumental reflections on the nature and use of history, Marc Bloch sounds a note of caution:

> History is neither watchmaking nor cabinet construction. . . . It is an endeavor toward a better understanding . . . which inevitably involves a rather large dose of personal opinion . . . as history struggles to penetrate beneath the mere surface of actions. . . . History has therefore been called the most difficult of sciences.[1]

Bloch reminds us that each science, taken by itself, represents but a fragment of the total reality. For that reason, when we consider the

Protestant movement in its historic sweep of 180 years in Latin American history, we are faced with a complex challenge. Protestant history is filled with both "sombras y luces;" "cavernas y cumbres" ["shadows and lights;" "caves and peaks."] We stand at a *kairos* moment. Harvey Cox reminds us in his preliminary paper for this conference that "just as the Panama Conference occurred at the cusp of the 19th and 20th centuries, this conference in San José gathers at the cusp of the 20th and 21st centuries." In contemporary Christian history, the fundamental southward shift of Christianity is an unquestioned reality. Latin American Protestant and Pentecostal growth form a significant part of the moving of the center of Christendom toward the South. Walbert Buhlman was prophetic only a few years ago in calling our attention to "The Coming of the Third Church."

How do we interpret the last eighty years with honesty and objectivity? Can we set those events and personalities within the context of the social, political, and economic realities of the Western Hemisphere during those years? Are there lessons we can learn from that pilgrimage that can help us on our journey in the coming years?

I believe that it is possible to unravel and reweave the threads of history, complex as they are, if we are willing to open our veins and inject into them some of both the pain and the vision of Protestantism's pioneers in Latin America.

With the concept, "writing by opening our veins," Frederick Buechner, contemporary author and Christian, suggests that historians perform a kind of "transfusion." They attempt to inject the experiences of others into the bloodstream of today's world. This we will attempt to do, following the example of the greatest of all missionaries, Paul of Tarsus. Paul wrote to the early Christians in Thessalonica, Greece, in 50 CE, recalling his deep personal involvement in mission:

> We had courage . . . to declare to you the gospel of God in spite of great opposition. . . . so we speak, not to please mortals, but to please God who tests our hearts. . . .we never came with words of flattery or with a pretext for greed. . . . we were gentle among you. . . . So deeply do we care for you that we are determined to share with you not only the gospel of God but also our selves."(I Thessalonians 2:1-8)

It is my opinion that a review of the past eighty years of ecumenical history in Latin America since the Panama Congress of 1916 is worth the effort only if we are willing to enter into the frustrations, the anguish, and the limitations of those years, as well as to celebrate their vision and triumphs.

The Latin America of Yesterday

We need to remember that Latin America was not considered of great importance by world historians until recent years. Arnold Toynbee, one of the greatest historians of this century, wrote very little, if anything, about Latin America. He visited Latin America only once, making a brief stop in Puerto Rico in 1962. However, he did say about that visit, "Hay cosas que estan pasando en America Latina hoy, cosas que, a mi juicio, podrian tener el significado en la historia que tuvo, en el pasado, el Renacimiento del siglo XV." [There are things happening in Latin America today, things that, in my judgment, could have the same historical significance as the Renaissance of the fifteenth century.] After using this quote in an address to the Committee on Cooperation in Latin America, John A. Mackay made the following comment: "Hay cosas que estan pasando en las iglesias latinoamericanas hoy, que podrian tener el mismo significado para la Iglesia Universal de Cristo y el movimiento ecumenico que en la historia tuvo la Reforma del siglo XVI, gracias a su redescubrimiento de la Biblia y el Evangelio de Cristo." [2]

[There are things happening in the churches of Latin America today that could have the same significance for the Universal Church of Christ and the ecumenical movement that the Reformation of the sixteenth century had in history, thanks to the rediscovery of the Bible and the gospel of Christ.]

Evangelical Christianity in Latin America was also seen to lie outside the purview of Christian history for many decades. It was viewed as an extension of Protestantism from North America, Britain, and Europe, much as Roman Catholicism in Latin America was seen as a projection of Ibero-Hispanic Catholicism in another continent. The uniqueness of Latin American Protestantism was not recognized until recent years. I venture to say that the world still has to discover Latin America as a world region and evangelical Christianity in Latin America in its unique historical dimensions.

Our task now is to place the ecumenical journey in Latin America within the context of world history and the history of Christianity.

The World and Latin America

Protestantism emerged in Latin America at a time when that region was seen to lie on the outskirts of world events. Latin America as a cultural and political entity was not recognized as such until the early 1900s. Before then, it was viewed merely as a source of cheap commodities for the First World. It was identified in literature as "South America," "Central America," "Mexico," or "the Caribbean," not as "Latin America." But, thanks to visionaries like José Vasconcellos and others, Latin Americans came to be identified by some as "a cosmic race" with many expressions of a unique culture and a political reality.

The indigenous peoples of Latin America were considered "relics of history," rather than a dynamic community that had been tragically brutalized by the dominant culture. Perhaps only in this decade of the five hundredth anniversary of the arrival of the first Europeans on the shores of the Western Hemisphere, have these indigenous communities reemerged before the world as the powerful force in Latin America's future that they had been in her past.

The contributions of African American religions have also been recognized in recent years and have enriched our understanding of Latin America's religious heritage. Walter Altmann has pointed out the rich religious pluralism of Latin America and the urgent need for oppressed peoples to own their unique religious backgrounds. As we approach the end of the second millennium of the Christian era, we have reached some degree of appreciation of the religious heritage of indigenous American religions, religious movements of African origin, and of the special contributions by both Roman Catholic and Protestant Christianity. But this was certainly not true eighty years ago when the Congress of Christian Work gathered in the Canal Zone in 1916.

Protestantism Within the Context of an Emerging Hemispheric Reality

Alberto Rembao, a prophet of Latin American Protestant identity, wrote about "the transculturation of Latin America."[3] He believed that the blending of the Hispanic, Indian, African, and European strains into a new racial and cultural reality called "the Latin American," was symbolic of new opportunities for the human race. He foresaw the growth of evangelical Christianity, the rise of popular movements of social change, and new world alliances that would bring Latin America into a more prominent role within the family of nations.

He also saw Protestantism as a renewing spiritual and cultural force with the potential of transforming a divided and segregated society into a new kind of human family. He coined the term "transculturation," which he determined to be a new cultural reality rising above its component cultural parts to form a new model of social integration.

Was this too lofty a dream? Is it possible that Christianity (without its aberrations of dogmatism and exclusivity) might still become a spiritual force uniting the diverse strains of Latin America into a new spiritual "race"?

As we attempt to look both backward and into the future, I suggest a vision for the twenty-first century which proclaims that

- the Christ who was born in Bethlehem will continue to invade these lands of palm, pine, and desert with his lifegiving words of hope and renewal
- the Word of God, spoken and incarnate, will continue to penetrate the most remote jungles and fetid *barrios de miseria* [slums] and bring holiness to revive the spirit of rural and urban masses
- the church of the living God will gather into her loving arms Latinos, Anglos, indigenous peoples, the sons and daughters of former slaves, and immigrants (now including those from the Pacific Rim)—all Latin Americans—and continue the work of transforming this heterogenous company into bearers of light and hope

Such a vision will require us to reach back through the past decades of tension, struggle, mistrust, and division to see the hand of God guiding a tiny Protestant community emerging to become part of the people of God. Our purpose here is to experience a "transfusion" of that vision and integrity of the past into our minds and hearts today.

The evangelical community in Latin America has a spiritual heritage to preserve and a challenge to meet in the twenty-first century. Our only claim to be a legitimate and vital part of the future of Latin America is that we present through word and deed the message that Jesus Christ is the sovereign Lord of all life.

To begin weaving the tapestry of the next century, we must unravel some of the strands of past decades and reweave them carefully so that the pattern is clearly understood.

The Christian community will continue to face the new colonialisms of today that militate against the liberation struggle.

Militarism, materialism, and racism will always lurk in the shadows. Long-term justice issues will not go away. "The Debt Jubilee," proposed by Christian leaders such as Archbishop Desmond Tutu, must be pressed at the highest levels. The new addiction to consumerism will be very powerful. Victims of economic structural adjustment will continue to cry out because 70 million children die each year as a result of those policies. Recent years have witnessed the largest transfer of wealth ever from the Third World to the First World. Equitable debt relief must be negotiated, the environment stabilized, and disempowerment through development arrested.

Yet the basic missionary task will continue to be much as it was in 1916, only with new challenges: How do we understand the context in which we are called to mission? What will be our response? How will the people of God respond *together* with a relevant ecumenical agenda?

Missionaries and Visionaries Who Pioneered Ecumenism

The historian Jacob Burckhardt made the following comment about pivotal historical personalities: "Los personajes historicos solo pueden ser comprendidos en todas sus dimensiones al tomarse en cuenta las realidades de su epoca y sus logros."[4] [The full dimension of historical characters can be understood only if one examines them and their achievements within the context and the realities of their times.] The pioneers of ecumenism must be evaluated in the light of the tremendous opposition that was mounted to thwart the cause of evangelical Christianity in the early years. We cannot pay high enough tribute to the early missionaries and the colporteurs of the Bible for their dogged determination, as well as their Christlike spirit. They knew how to make friends and cultivate friendships. They must be judged in the light of all the adversity that surrounded them. Someone has written that the nine-year journey of James Thomson (1816-1825) can only be compared, in terms of its permanent effect on a continent, to the travels of St. Paul in the first Christian century.

Ross Kinsler has wisely referred to the Protestant movement (1846-1996) as the second spiritual conquest of Latin America, following the first conquest by Roman Catholic Christianity beginning in 1492. Evangelical pioneers were men and women of vision, far ahead of their times even in their countries and churches of origin. They lived with courage, integrity, and personal piety in the finest of the Christian missionary tradition. Not only do we pay tribute to the missionaries sent by denominational boards but also to the para-ecclesial agencies such as the Bible societies, the YMCA, and the YWCA.

Pioneer agencies such as the YMCA began work in Buenos Aires in 1870, Brazil in 1887, and Mexico City in 1891. They opened doors to understanding and service in environments hostile to societal change and social innovation. Their leaders were men and women who were convinced that ecumenical planning and action were not only practical but mandated by the gospel. Those early YMCA leaders were present at the Panama Congress in 1916. Their voices joined others there and, in later years, in Montevideo, Havana , Buenos Aires, and Lima. Today we render tribute to leaders such as Erasmo Braga of Brazil, Gonzalo Baez Camargo of Mexico, and Sante Uberto Barbieri of Argentina, who proposed in the first half of this century a program to respond in evangelical terms to the vast spiritual and physical needs of Latin America.

Now we turn to the more difficult aspect of Latin American ecumenical history: the liberal "project" vs. the task of evangelization. This was a central theme at Panama.

The Liberal Project

José Miguez Bonino in *Faces of Latin American Protestantism* has painted a clear portrait of "the liberal face" (the liberal project) that was a dominant theme of the 1916 Congress of Christian Work. "But which liberal project?" asks Miguez. "I believe it was an ambiguous event in which there were differences, divergences, and contradiction."[5] For example, he describes two currents of thought present at Panama: One was reflected in Report 2 in a statement about "aggressive commercial agents, the plundering type of concessionaires, overbearing, arrogant industrial managers and bosses, swaggering tourists, ill-bred consular representatives and diplomats . . . and, occasionally, condescending missionaries."[6] The other current was the benevolent version of Pan-Americanism expressed by the growing relationship between the United States and Latin America in educational, social, and religious services. The Committee on Cooperation in Latin America (CCLA) was certainly caught between these two realities as it tried to develop mission strategy in the 1920s. Fortunately, CCLA Hispanic staff members Alberto Rembao, Gonzalo Baez Camargo, Jorge Howard, and others, kept this dialogue alive between the Americas.

Miguez writes clearly about "the incoherences of Panama and Montevideo" but also pleads with us today to "unravel the threads . . . and reknit, on the loom of a different historical moment, a new social and theological understanding."[7] He is convinced that we can recover some of the threads of "the liberal project": the Protestant inheritance of freedom and self-identity, the responsibility of the person in solidarity with the community, the autonomy of human reason in building the earthly city, and the rationality of hope in a history of which Jesus Christ is Lord.[8] Perhaps Ruben Alves is right when he states that Protestantism can be properly understood as the only successful export, ever, from United States to Latin America!

We need to reclaim some of the heritage of a utopian Protestantism and reinterpret and relive in our time a renewed hope for those who are marginalized in our societies. This should be our response to the supposed "end of history" and our vote to construct a new historical project for Protestantism.

The dynamic Latin American leadership of the early part of this century was in touch, both emotionally and spiritually, with ecumenical leaders in North America and Europe. Given even the cultural baggage that most Anglos and Españoles brought with them, the transparent motivation of Robert E. Speer, John A. Mackay, W. Stanley Rycroft, Juan Ortz Gonzalez, Julio Navarro Monzón, N. B. Foster Stockwell, Charles J. Ewald, and Harry and Susan Strachan won the respect and affection of Latin Americans. They had to struggle against the missionary mentality of a North American messianism which held that the saviors of Latin America would come from the North!

Those expatriate missionary leaders knew they had feet of clay, yet they lived out their lives with both pastoral and prophetic zeal. All had their foibles and limitations, but history looks back on their lives and ministry with awe and profound appreciation.

Mileposts

We can trace three general periods of ecumenical development. First, there was the period (before 1929) that Julio de Santa Ana has called "interdenominational Protestantism." Before the Havana Conference in 1929, there had been little input from Latin Americans to the ecumenical agenda. It was a period in which the North American mission boards were putting their own houses in order, to be able to deal honestly and openly with Latin American churches. They were slow to step aside so that Latin American leadership could assume control. The newly formed Committee on Cooperation in Latin America was instrumental in keeping the U.S. mission boards engaged in ecumenical cooperation during the 1920s. However, it seems that denominationalism and paternalism frequently determined their actions.

The significant change came in 1929 in Havana, when Latin American leaders, especially from the Caribbean, took bold steps to claim the ecumenical movement as their own. The Cuban Methodist Luis Alonso expressed the process of the Latinization of Protestantism in these words: "América Latina será salvada solamente por los latinoamericanos, en el amplio sentido del concept . . . hasta que no se haya "latinizada" adquiriendo normas y caracteres de acuerdo con la gente que desea servir."[9] [Latin America will have been saved by Latin Americans, in the full sense of the concept . . . when it is no longer "latinized," acquiring norms and characteristics according to those it wishes to serve.]

In the decade of the 1930s the Protestant community witnessed the emergence of youth and student movements that were made up of second- and third-generation Protestants. The doors to a university education, as well as possibilities for social involvement, began to open for Protestants. A clearer understanding of inter-American tensions and economic exploitation was being articulated. Programs of Christian education and social ministry began to evolve despite a significant reduction in missionary funds due to the financial crisis in the United States. Latin American civil strife and World War II postponed plans for further continental meetings until the Havana Youth Conference of 1946 and the First Latin America Evangelical Conference in 1949.

During the second state of ecumenical development (1929-1961), Latin American Protestants experienced *una toma de conscienzia* [a deep personal awareness] of Protestant identity and gained the sense of a movement that went beyond only "interdenominational cooperation." John A. Mackay's *The Other Spanish Christ,* written in 1932, signaled a new era in which Protestantism was understood to be a legitimate part of the Latin American religious landscape.[10] Lay-inspired ecumenical movements like ULAJE [Latin American Union of Evangelical (Protestant) Youth], ISAL [Church and Society in Latin America], and CELADEC [Latin American Commission on Christian Education] brought Protestants together around issues in church and society. It was clearly evident after Lima (1961) and Buenos Aires II (1969) that there was a growing ecumenical consciousness in Latin America.

This third phase of ecumenism (after 1961) showed respect for the diversity of responses to the evangelical challenge in Latin America. An incarnational approach took precedence over one that was more doctrinaire. Outworn imported labels such as "liberal," "fundamentalist," "conservative," and "progressive" were gradually put aside. A new Protestant consensus began to emerge.

While the denominations with historic roots in the Reformation developed effective working relationships, cooperation among the newer denominations emerged after 1948 through joint programs of literature production, mass communications, and evangelism. These newer evangelical movements that had sprung from the Holiness, Keswick, and Pentecostal movements began to relate with confidence to both the newer denominations and the historic Protestant churches. It was at the twenty-fifth anniversary of the Latin American Biblical Seminary in Costa Rica in 1948 that this movement began to coalesce. One hundred sixty-five former students gathered from fifteen countries to renew friendships and plan joint activities for the 1950s.

Meanwhile in the non-Latin Caribbean in the 1960s, as new nations in the Caribbean basin achieved their independence, a similar process of ecumenical development brought into being CADEC, (Christian Action for Development in the Caribbean), an organization that included Roman Catholics and was the precursor of what is today the Caribbean Conference of Churches (CCC). The British and European orientation of the churches in the Caribbean created unique ecumenical challenges.

Many of these strains of ecumenical endeavor, called by a variety of names, merged in Oaxtepec, Mexico, in 1978 to form the Latin American Council of Churches (CLAI). Above all, the third phase of ecumenical cooperation began to build bridges with popular movements in society. Today we are reaping some of the fruits of that intentional shift to identify with the agenda of the masses. But the ecumenical movement had inner weaknesses that we cannot ignore. I shall attempt to point these out:

- The movement was male dominated and included few women in positions of leadership, except in the youth and student movements.

- It was elitist in the sense that a small leadership pool tended to dominate meetings. The alliance of much of the missionary community with the neoliberal establishment shielded the movement from understanding structures of injustice. Many missionaries had been formed ideologically as part of the middle or upper-middle classes in the United States during the 1950s and 1960s.
- The movement was largely bereft of "the marginalized," such as indigenous persons, workers, and peasants. The "immigrant churches" were often poorly represented.
- The movement depended heavily on financial support from mission boards. This was true of both conciliar and other cooperative movements.

However, given those limitations, it was a time of remarkable achievement by a movement that had to deal with vast distances, cultural disparities, theological dissonance, personality clashes, financial limitations, and, above all, the ever present specter of inter-American tensions. In the face of such problems, we can be cheered by the words of the noted anthropologist and Episcopal layperson, Margaret Mead. She once said of the ecumenical movement, "It is a sociological impossibility."[11]

Issues and Strategies

I invite you now to think about the content of ecumenical dialogue and program that developed over the eight decades:

The Legitimacy of the Protestant Witness to Christianity. First of all, there was the issue of the legitimacy of Protestantism in "Roman Catholic lands." How the term "Roman Catholic lands" in the religious sense was ever attached to Brazil, Mexico, or Colombia we may never know. But the terminology began with the assumption that the kings of Spain and Portugal and the Pope bestowed upon themselves the right to claim for God and the church the lands discovered by their armies and colonized by their merchants. The view of Latin America held by most people in the early part of this century was that those countries were the territory of a particular religious institution. This concept infiltrated the thinking of much Protestant missionary thinking. The struggle for "Protestant legitimacy," which began at the Edinburgh Conference of 1910, was largely won by North Americans and Latin Americans at Panama in 1916, but it was not until 1928, at the World Missionary Conference in Jerusalem, that a Latin American delegation was formally recognized as representing a region for mission work such as, for example, Africa or Asia.

Protestantism Can Flourish in Latin Culture. An idea promoted by certain Roman Catholic leaders was that something in the culture of Latin America made Protestantism "inadaptable al alma latinoamericana . . . una religion extranjerizante . . . una religion del alma anglosajona. El catolicismo es del alma latina . . . "[12] [Protestantism . . . cannot be adapted to the Latin American soul. . . . It is a religion that will introduce foreign customs (will lead Latin Americans to act like foreigners, adopt foreign ways). . . . It is a religion of the Anglo-Saxon soul. Catholicism is of the Latin soul]. It took the pens of Alberto Rembao and John A. Mackay to challenge that thinking and to show that evangelical Christianity can put down roots and grow in Latin soil just as well as coffee and banana trees. Some day, Protestant Christianity will become just as much a part of Latin horizons as the Andes Mountains and the Argentine pampas.

Protestantism as a Positive Factor in Inter-American Relations. A third issue promoted in the 1940s by a segment of North American clerics was that Protestantism was having a detrimental effect on inter-American relations. Articles appeared attacking Protestant missionaries and the funding of missionary activities as a threat to the "Good Neighbor Policy." Thanks to leaders such as Jorge Howard and his book *Religious Liberty in Latin America*, the mood began to change. It should be noted that the Committee on Cooperation in Latin America mailed a copy of Howard's book to each member of the United States Congress.

It is difficult to imagine in 1997 the rhetoric and prejudice of an earlier time that sought to exclude one of the three major Christian confessions from the Latin lands of the Americas. But the evidence of clerical bigotry and diplomatic propaganda is a part of history.

The Irruption of the Poor: the Voices of the Voiceless. "The excluded" and "the voiceless"—women, indigenous people, workers, and peasants—were seldom a part of ecumenical activities, except perhaps as objects of concern. Never as actors. It was not until the growth of popular Protestant movements and the participation of major Pentecostal denominations that those excluded sectors of society began to have a voice. Perhaps the Declaration of Barbados, related to the evangelization of indigenous people (1960s), was the first strong statement that awakened the Protestant movement to the legitimate concerns of indigenous people about the strategies of Catholic and Protestant missions. Today's "option for the excluded ones" is a concept that moves us beyond "the option for the poor," as expressed by the Second Vatican Council in the early 1960s. We are challenged now to stand on a new frontier with all the excluded ones.

Women: Reclaiming Their Rightful Place. The role of women, not only in Latin American life but within Protestantism as a whole, has too often been a reflection more of the culture than of the gospel. Latin women have carried "burdens" for too long, as poignantly expressed by Nelly Ritchie:

> The campesina woman, stooped over the land from which she may be able to extract food for her children; the woman who from early morning carries buckets of water, washes the clothes . . . cares for the children; the woman bent double in the factory, close to others but not knowing them, selling her work strength; the woman in the home, trying to respond to all the requirements of a labor not recognized by others. These are women exhausted by double exploitation: that which goes with being an oppressed people and that of being a woman."[13]

Elsa Tamez has written much about the efforts of women to join the liberation struggle. Here are some of her words: "Latin American women along with our male companions want to recreate cultural, ecclesiastical and theological history. Together we want to cure 'the open wounds of Latin America'. . . . Many Latin American women know that when they take their first steps to join history and to be protagonists, they cannot turn back."[14]

The churches' agenda for the next millennium must place in the forefront the role and contribution of women.

Vatican II Challenges Roman Catholicism. The Second Vatican Council (1959-1965) challenged Protestants as well as Roman Catholics to catch up with the times. Protestants had only one observer from Latin America, the visionary Methodist theologian, José Míguez Bonino. We owe much to him for his interpretation of the council's work to Latin American evangelicals.

The Christian world—Catholic, Orthodox, and Protestant—is still being shaken by the recommendations of Vatican II. Its far-reaching implications have yet to be fully understood. However, in Latin America in the 1960s it was reassuring to hear words such as the following: "Protestants are now only separated brothers and sisters in the Christian family." That simple yet profound statement opened up possibilities for new relationships between all Christians in Latin America around common issues of witness and service. Many progressive Catholics in Latin America suffered during the 1970s and 1980s as they tried to be faithful to the new directions laid out by Vatican II. Evangelicals and Roman Catholics did come closer together amid the sufferings of the post-Vatican II era. But many deep wounds and scars still remain from past centuries of intolerance and religious discrimination. Can we begin to ask forgiveness from each other?

New Opportunities to Forgive. Let us use an example from the Czech Republic, where a dramatic step was taken in 1995 upon the canonization of Jan Sarkander. Sarkander, a Catholic priest, was put to death by Protestant officials in 1620 during the violent re-Catholicization of the Bohemian people in the seventeenth century. His canonization, interpreted by Catholics as priestly fidelity in the midst of martyrdom, was seen by Reformed Christians as a contemporary reaffirmation of the violence done to them in the past. While no suitable solution was found to satisfy either side, perhaps the period before the year 2000 will be a time of grace and a time to ask pardon. Pope John Paul II took the initiative in a homily: "I as Pope of the Church of Rome, in the name of all Catholics, ask forgiveness for the wrongs inflicted on non-Catholics during the turbulent history of these people." Recently in the Czech Republic, a commission of Catholics and members of the Reformed tradition was formed to study that period of history. As we enter the next millennium, cannot we, too, speak and accept words asking forgiveness for past wrongs between Christians?[15]

Evangelical Christianity still has to deal with the impact within Roman Catholicism of Vatican II and the Medellín conference of 1968. Traditional parish and monolithic religious structures were seriously challenged, but those new thrusts were often blunted by a conservative hierarchy. I believe it is too early to assess the long-term impact of Vatican II. Here is an assessment by the aged Benedictine monk Godfrey Diekmann, a prominent figure in Vatican II: "Vatican

II is by far the most radical, the most productive, and the most challenging document in the whole history of the Church, and we weren't ready for it. . . . I think what we are suffering now as Roman Catholics is a collective stomach ache. We swallowed too much!"[16]

In the spirit of Vatican II, Catholics and Protestants alike must continue to take initiatives to right the wrongs of past intolerance and to ask probing questions of each other about the mission of the church in the coming millennium.

The Power of Pentecostalism within Evangelical Christianity. The rapid growth of Pentecostalism as a major force in evangelical Christianity in Latin America has caused the ecumenical movement to pause and reflect. The majority of Protestants in Latin America belong to some form of Pentecostalism. The Pentecostal movement reminds us that the Christian life is one of joy, transformation, and complete commitment to God. The message of the gospel is about freedom from sin, both individual and collective. The Pentecostal movement reminds us of the prophetic nature of Christ's ministry and the apocalyptic dimensions of both our responsible participation in history and the ultimate triumph of the forces of good over evil.

Pentecostalism is a challenge to the historic denominations, both theologically and historically. We must repent of caricatures and indifference toward Pentecostals. We have not given due attention to the work of the Holy Spirit outside our traditional denominations.

The rapid dissemination of Pentecostal beliefs has produced vibrant alternatives in the dominant culture by changing relationships within family, community, and workplace. Traditional Protestants have been thrown back upon their heritage of evangelical piety to ask themselves what happened to "the joy of our salvation," the centrality of Scripture, and the nature of the evangelistic task.

How do we historic Protestants reknit the threads of yesterday into the fabric of modernity? Did we miss something in the liberal project of yesterday, the bold affirmation of individual and God-given rights, the pact into which we entered for the common welfare? Have we lost the joy, exuberance, mystery, and spiritual power of the invasion of the Spirit into our lives and churches? Has Pentecostalism come upon the religious scene to weave again the threads of personal piety and community-building into the fabric of Protestant identity and mission? Can Pentecostalism help bring about a rebirth of the original liberal project that ignited a new day for Latin America a century and a half ago, when evangelical seed began to sprout in Latin soil?

Ecclesiology, Ethics, and the "Public Church." We come now to the ecclesiological challenge in the ecumenical dialogue of our times. If we are to become participants in God's activity in history, this dialogue pushes us, as churches, more and more into the ethical arena. We must ask ourselves as denominations if we are structured more to defend denominational traditions than to participate in God's ongoing activity in the world. The church has great untapped reserves as a "public church"—reserves it has avoided using in the defense of human and civil rights. It is true that Protestantism has taken pride in its ability to become involved in justice struggles, and it would like to believe that it is not wedded to vested interests. But, sadly, we are often more interested in defending our denominational past than in taking our place in the emerging ecumenical future.

The Next Millennium in Historical Perspective

We are proud that it was the missionary vocation that thrust the ecumenical movement into the world to proclaim the gospel amid the religious pluralism of the twentieth century. Early in the first millennium, in 49 CE, it was that same Macedonian call which the Apostle Paul heard in Troas and which sent him out beyond the established boundaries of his own culture, social class, and geographic region. Today, at the dawn of the third millennium, we continue to be challenged by mission to cross all kinds of frontiers—spiritual, cultural, geographic.

Are we willing today to consider some fundamental adaptations of the missionary movement in the twenty-first century that will thrust us toward the dispersed and excluded sectors of modern society? Can we leave behind an institutionally based movement and identify ourselves with the voiceless and the excluded? Are we willing to challenge the male bias in our churches and thus free the largest excluded sector, women, to exercise full rights and responsibilities in the mission of the church? If we are not, then a male-dominated movement in mission will lead the church back into another "Dark Age" of spiritual poverty and ingrown leadership. Can the church challenge the social order, as well as church polity, and lift women into positions of leadership on a par with men?

The rate of change will only accelerate in the next decade. The cybernetic age assures us of a communication explosion. The United Nations will be recast to address changing relations between superpowers. The document of the World Council of Churches, "Toward a Common Understanding and Vision," calls upon its member churches to explore new models for a world forum of Christian organizations. In Latin America we should be ready for surprises in relationships between Christians. We must move forward with open hearts and open minds. Basic points of caution, valid in the past, are worth listening to once again: we must avoid confessional isolation, denominational rigidity, and empire building. The denominations have also learned that authentic ecumenical involvement is in no way incompatible with genuine confessional commitment.

I suggest that from the perspective of service and mission we must move, intentionally and dramatically, toward other sectors in society. The problem of human misery must be addressed both structurally and in terms of human compassion, so that "the church of the excluded" may become the beachhead of a new mission advance in the next millennium.

The same dramatic initiatives are required from the perspective of Faith and Order. Theology is still important. Effective church structures are still vital to doing God's work in the world. Churches must be so structured that each congregation can become a center for community renewal rather than a "refuge of the masses."

A major part of the mission of the CCLA in the next decade may well be to become an organizing agent for Christian organizations, helping them pool their efforts to move the church beyond personal evangelism and church planting of the twentieth century. It was that missionary vocation, placed by the ecumenical movement in the midst of a world, loved by God in the plurality of culture and religions, which has always challenged the church to take the gospel beyond established boundaries. It can happen again in the next millennium.

Conclusion

In Panama in 1916, the Protestant missionary movement stood not only at the physical crossroads of the Americas but at a crucial moment in the Christian history of the Americas. With the inspiration of the Holy Spirit, steps were taken to preach and live the gospel within the context of Latin American realities. That first meeting of

Christians from the North and the South gave life to a movement of Christian fraternity that still has an impact on our lives. In Panama there was a serious attempt to set aside denominational agendas and missionary paternalism and embark on a new venture of ecumenical cooperation.

We stand here, eighty years later, with a similar opportunity to preach the same gospel in a different context. Will we use the experience that history offers us to plan wisely and courageously for the next millennium? Let us remember that The Acts of the Apostles is still the book in the Bible that has never been completed!

End Notes

1. Marc Bloch, *The Art of the Historian* (1956), pp. 12,14.
2. John A. Mackay, Address to the Committee on Cooperation in Latin America (1963).
3. Cf. Alberto Rembao, *Discurso a la nación evangelica* (1949).
4. Jacob Burckhardt, *Reflexiones sobre la historia universal* (1905).
5. Cf. José Miguez Bonino, *Faces of Latin American Protestantism* (1995).
6. Report of the Panama Congress, vol. 2, p. 41.
7. Miguez Bonino, *Faces*, p. 23.
8. Ibid, p. 24.
9. Report of the Havana Conference of 1929, *Hacia la renovación hispanoamericana* (1930).
10. Cf. John A. Mackay, *The Other Spanish Christ* (1933). Spanish editions in 1953, 1988, 1991, and 1994.
11. John H. Sinclair, *Juan A. Mackay: Un escoces con alma latina* (1991, p. 193).
12. Cf. Toribio Esquivel Obregon, *El protestantismo en Mexico* (1946).
13. Dow Kirkpatrick, ed., *Faith Born in the Struggle of Life* (1988), pp. 88, 91.
14. Ibid., p. 191.
15. Ecumenical Press Service, "Ecumenical Challenges," (1997), p. 19.
16. *Minneapolis Star Tribune,* March 9, 1997.

Hunger for God, Hunger for Bread, Hunger for Humanity: A Southern Perspective

Jung Mo Sung

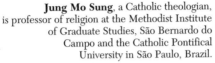

Jung Mo Sung, a Catholic theologian, is professor of religion at the Methodist Institute of Graduate Studies, São Bernardo do Campo and the Catholic Pontifical University in São Paulo, Brazil.

All attempts to analyze any social reality presuppose three questions: From which position does one speak? For whom does one speak? Why does one speak?

My analysis comes from Latin America, and, even more specifically, from the perspective of the majority of the poor population. It is important to begin with this affirmation, for there is another paper, dealing with the same issue, written from the perspective of the North. Furthermore, this text is written for members of Christian churches with the purpose of discussing and debating the challenges that the American continents present to the mission of the church and the responses that we can hope for from the Gospel. Therefore, my central objective is not to grapple with technical questions, but, rather, to address the pressing spiritual questions that currently stir our continent.

Social Apartheid

The American continents, as we all know, are not culturally homogeneous. A first look reveals two distinct blocs: North America (in this analysis meaning the United States and Canada) and Latin America (Mexico, Central America, the Caribbean, and South America). But in both blocs we find similarities. Among these, the most obvious is the great concentration of wealth[1] in contrast to extreme poverty: in Latin America, between pockets of wealth in a sea of poverty; in Canada and the United States, between pockets of poverty in a sea of wealth .

A new factor within this social contrast, which in one form or another has always existed on these continents, is the separation between these two social groups of rich and poor—to such a degree that some analysts call it "social apartheid." According to Hugo Assmann, "The *primary factor* in the present world situation is certainly the terrible power of the logic of exclusion and the growing insensitivity of most persons in relationship to it."[2]

Increasing numbers of people in the United States and the majority of people in Latin America are excluded from the marketplace. This means that they are excluded not only from the fruits of development, but often from the conditions that make possible a life of dignity—sometimes from survival itself. Exclusion from the marketplace does not mean, however, exclusion from society and from the reach of those means of communication that create in the excluded the same desires for consumer goods that drive the rest of the population. Therefore we have a tragic situation in which the poor—both youth and adults—are stimulated to desire sophisticated and superfluous consumer goods at the same time that they are denied the possibility of acquiring the basic necessities for dignified survival.

One of the basic reasons for this process of exclusion is, without a doubt, the structural unemployment that affects the two continents and, indeed, almost the entire world. We call the present unemployment "structural" because it is not the result of an economic recession that will end or be eased by economic growth. On the contrary, the profits of large businesses are increasing and their stock is rising precisely because they are reducing their personnel. The wealthy countries that belong to the Organization for Economic Cooperation and Development (OCDE) now have almost 40 million unemployed workers.

This structural unemployment is a result of the present model of economic globalization and of the technological revolution. According to Peter Drucker, "In the industrial economy production [has] ceased being 'connected' to employment, and the movement of capital, and not of trade (whether goods or services) [has become] the driving force of the world economy."[3]

This process can be seen as the coronation of an inversion in capitalism, described by Max Weber in his famous book, *The Protestant Ethic and the Spirit of Capitalism:* "Man is dominated by the production of money, by acquisition seen as the ultimate purpose of his life. Economic acquisition is no longer subordinated by man as a means of satisfying his material necessities. This inversion which we can define as a natural relationship, so irrational from a naive point of views, is evidently a guiding principle of capitalism."[4]

In premodern societies people worked to live. In modern, capitalist societies they live to accumulate wealth. In our day, characterized by the globalized economy, technological revolution, and new administrative methods that have greatly increased productivity, programs to decrease employment have created even greater profit for businesses and more income for stock holders and executives. Furthermore, the financial system—which should be linked to the service system—has increased and become more important, and is, to a large degree, disconnected from production. Wealth is financialized and, to a large degree, fictitious—a matter less of tangible goods than of numbers blinking on a computer screen.

This unlimited desire, this unlimited search for wealth, creates two serious unintentional effects. The first is the threat to the ecological system. The voracious search for greater profits is destroying an ecological system that has developed over billions of years. The very possibility of human life is threatened. The second effect is the serious social crisis in our countries: not just immense social contrasts between rich and poor, but also unbridled violence and the growing traffic in drugs.

We must add two other important facts in order to understand better the particularly dramatic reality of Latin America. The first is that being unemployed or poor in countries that are making drastic cuts in their few and inefficient social programs is vastly different from being unemployed or poor in rich countries with functioning social programs. The second is that in almost all Latin American countries we find "different juxtapositions of time and space." Within the same country different social groups live in different historical times. Some live in a premodern culture, using methods of production introduced centuries ago at the time of the agricultural revolution, without access to the formal education of industrialized urban societies. Others belong to the era of the Industrial Revolution, especially as developed by Ford. Still others live in a postmodern or postindustrial culture with the latest technological developments. This disjunction of time causes serious economic problems. Many people want to work but do not have the skills for the few vacancies existing in the businesses that are modernizing in order to compete in the market place.

Together with this disjunction of time there is the serious problem of "spacial distancing." The elite of Latin countries feel closer to, and identify with, the elite of the wealthy Northern countries, rather than the great majority of their own poor population. In a sense, the Latin elite feel that they belong to the consumer community of the world marketplace, not to their own countries, their own national societies. In this kind of situation it is increasingly difficult to obtain the support of the middle and upper sectors of Latin American society for programs and policies that seek to alleviate pressing social problems.

A Culture of Insensitivity

A society based on the logic of exclusion creates, and, at the same time, is fed by, a culture of insensitivity. It is sad to say that we can prove in our daily activities a growing insensitivity to the suffering of others, particularly the poor. Not even the continued assassination of children who live in the streets shocks us. After all, those children are poor!

This culture of insensitivity, bordering on cynicism, does not develop by chance. It is the fruit of diverse historical, social, and anthropological factors. Given limited time and space, I will cite only some of the more compelling ones.

Within our societies there is a concept of the inevitability of inequality and social exclusion. This thesis received a great stimulus with the destruction of the communist bloc. Lacking an alternative model, the thesis that capitalism, with its neoliberal ideology, represented the "end of history"[5] gained an impetus never before imagined. With the dissemination of the thesis that there was no feasible alternative, the present social situation began to be seen as inevitable.

Not only inevitable, it was also seen as just. Growing among us is what John Kenneth Galbraith called the "culture of contentment": the idea that the "good" integrated into the marketplace "are doing nothing less than profiting from their just rewards," and, therefore, "if good fortune is merited, or if it is a reward for personal merit, there is no plausible justification for any action that prejudices or inhibits or reduces that which is or can be enjoyed."[6] The other side of the coin is that the poor are seen as guilty of their own poverty and that they are receiving *their* just rewards. Therefore, the present concentrated and excluding mechanisms of the marketplace are seen as "incarnations" of a transcendental judge and justice. These market mechanisms are a secularized version of the theology of retribution, so criticized by Jesus and by the reformers through the theology of grace. In a more ecclesiastical setting, a modern religious version exists as the "theology of prosperity."

This social inequality began to be perceived by the majority as not only inevitable and just, but even as beneficial. Here we have proof of how neoliberalism managed to become the dominant ideology of our time. For neoliberals, who have an unwavering faith in the ability of the marketplace to solve economic and social problems, the intensifying of exclusion and social inequalities is a good sign. Inequality for them is the motor of economic progress because it provides an incentive for competition among people and is, at the same time, the result of a society based on competition. Furthermore, the social crisis that is always seen by neoliberals as transitory would be for them a dual sign of progress, suggesting 1) that the economy is proceeding along the approved track of deregulation and 2) that society is moving toward the end of the state's intervention in the economy.

Based on the error of confusing economic growth with human and social development, current cultural and economic leaders suggest that modernization of the economy and of all society is the only way to proceed. Modernization is understood to mean the confining of discussion and action in the political and economic realm within the boundaries of instrumental reason, that is, of pragmatic concerns. Such confinement would require removal from the discussion of all human and social values, of all the rights and responsibilities of people and nations that, in a logical and chronological sense, existed long before the market economy. It would call for reducing everything to a question of greatest efficiency, given the reality of scarce means, and the desire for unlimited accumulation of wealth.

This is why Brazil's ex-Minister of Economy Roberto Campos, an arduous defender of neoliberalism, says that modernization, the only viable road for Latin America, "presuppose[s] a *cruel mystique* of effort and of a cult of efficiency."[7]

He speaks of a "cruel mystique," an expression that few Christians succeed in understanding. A mystique is a mysterious aura or force. How can it be cruel and good at the same time? Neoliberals seem to use it as a force for overcoming sin. And what is the principal sin for neoliberals? For them the basic cause of economic and social evils— original sin, in religious terms—is the economists' "pretension of understanding"[8] the marketplace, leading to all interventions of the state and of social movements. According to the economist Friedrich von Hayek and his followers, the impossibility of understanding the marketplace results in the impossibility of seeking conscious and intentional solutions for economic and social problems. That is, we human beings should abandon the desire of building a better society because every time we try, we end up intervening in the marketplace through the state or through civil actions, in well-meaning but unsuccessful attempts to mitigate unemployment and social inequality.

The only road left to us, according to the neoliberals, is to have faith in the "invisible hand" of the marketplace and to see the sufferings of the unemployed and the excluded as "necessary sacrifices" demanded by its laws. That is why the mystique that should help us overcome "the temptation of doing good"—title of a work by Peter Drucker[9]—appears to be "cruel." This cruel mystique is accompanied by worship—not of the God of mercy and life but of the efficiency of the marketplace.

The Good News of a God Who Is Love

In a world caught up in the "idolatry of the marketplace,"[10] what should be the mission of the Christian church? What "good news" should we announce in order to be faithful to the gospel?

First we must make clear that criticism of the idolatry of the marketplace does not mean criticism of the marketplace, as such, but of its sanctification, of absolute subjection to its laws.

We must unmask the sin of idolatry. We must unveil the spirit of idol worship—the worship of work, of human and social actions and relationships undertaken solely for the accumulation of wealth and for the purpose of unlimited consumption. We must show that the root of all economic and social ills is not our struggle to live in a more humane and just society, but, rather, as the Apostle Paul taught us, that "the love of money is a root of all kinds of evil" (1 Timothy 6:10).

We must reestablish a simple and irrefutable truth: the economy should exist to serve the lives of all. People should not be impelled to abide by economic laws designed solely for the accumulation of wealth. This is one of the most important ways of translating into today's language a profound teaching of Jesus: "The sabbath was made for humankind, and not humankind for the sabbath" (Mark 2:27).

The people of the Americas, the excluded ones in our societies, not only have hunger for bread but, also, for their denied humanity and for God. They are hungry for God, who excludes no one (Acts 10:35 and Romans 2:11) and who is among human beings "that they

40

may have life, and have it abundantly" (John 10:10). If this good news is to bear fruit in our society, we of the church must engage in a basic theological task: a critique of the theology of retribution, which is another facet of the "culture of contentment" and the "theology of prosperity." For they make sacred the injustice "of the world," revealing a god (idol) that legitimizes the culture of insensitivity and blames the victims of the mechanisms of exclusion in our society. This is why the theology of retribution must be replaced with the theology of grace: to show that God is not the cause of suffering and injustice, nor the provider of the minority's wealth; to announce that God's name cannot be used in vain to undergird injustice and cynicism. This replacement is necessary because God does not save us because of our merit but by grace. And if we want to live in accordance with this grace of God, we must look with gratitude beyond the logic of the marketplace and recognize the right of all people to a good and dignified life. In other words, we must reclaim the values of solidarity and equality.

In sociological terms we are speaking of a society in which everyone has a place. It is a world with room for many smaller worlds, where those who are different—"the Jews and the Gentiles"—learn to respect each other's differences and the right of everyone to a life of dignity. Without a doubt, the marketplace will be an important part of this society. But, just as surely, it will not be either a sanctified or an omnipotent marketplace. There must be state and social mechanisms of control that will complement the mechanisms of the market place, so that the basic rights of all people will be respected and ecological systems will be preserved.

To struggle for a society in which everyone has a place means not making one's political-economic agenda a criterion for judging among a variety of global or even partisan projects. In more immediate terms, it means to struggle on two fronts for the creation of more jobs and other economic mechanisms in order to generate income for the excluded sectors of society. The first of these two fronts is the political struggle to reform the state, enabling it to recover the political will for solving social problems and the economic ability to establish social programs and to intervene in, and give direction to, the economy. In this political struggle we must not forget the basic task of strengthening the civil society. It should act as a counterpoint to the state, combating the state's tendency to become bureaucratic and corrupt and to serve only the dominant elite. The second front is that of training workers in new techniques of production, helping them to create new kinds of economic activities such as, for example, cooperative or social industries. This training should be implemented by a system of formal public education— thus returning us to the problem of the state and the processes of popular or informal education.

These few indicators have been presented not to exhaust the matter but to help us remember that we must "incarnate" the good news of Jesus in the historical conditions of our own day. In closing, I want to point out another important fact: In a globalized world, solutions for problems cannot be thought of only in local or national terms. It is necessary to have linkages and coordination along international lines. This is another area in which Christian churches can offer a great service to humanity. Christian churches and international ecumenical organizations are among the few institutions that have both international and local networks. Furthermore, they are concerned about the lives of the poor and excluded. It is up to us to use these infrastructures and connections in the best and most creative ways, so that life, the "breath of the Spirit" which lives in all human beings, the great gift of God, can be defended with dignity and integrity.

End Notes

1. The wealth has become so concentrated that 358 billionaires in the world control more wealth than the national income of countries comprising 45 percent of the world's population.
2. Hugo Assmann. "Por una sociedad donde quepan todos," ed. José Duque (Quarta Jornada Teológica de CETELA, 10-13/07/95). San José: DEI, 1996, p. 380.
3. Peter Drucker. "As mudanças na economia mundial, *Politica Externa*, vol.1, n. 3, Dec. 92, São Paulo: Paz e Terra, p. 17 (original in English, 1989), This author is considered to be the "guru of gurus" in the administration of businesses.
4. Max Weber. *A ética protestante e o espiritu do capitalism*, 3rd ed. (São Paulo: Liv. Pioneira, 1983), p.33.
5. F. Fukuyama, *O fim da história e o último homen* (Rio de Janeiro: Rocco, 1992).
6. John Kenneth Galbraith. *A cultura do contentamento* (São Paulo: Pioneira, 1992), p. 12.
7. Roberto Campos. *Além do cotidano* (Rio de Janeiro: Record, 2nd ed., 1985).
8. Friedrich A. von Hayek. "A pretensão do conhecimento," *Humanidades*, vol. 2 n. 5, Oct-Dec. 1983, Brasília: UnB, pp. 47-54. An address given by Hayek on the occasion of receiving the Nobel Prize for economics,
9. Peter F. Drucker. *A tentação de fazer o bem* (Rio de Janeiro: Rocco, 1986).
10. See, for example, H. Assmann and F. Hinkelammert, *Idolotria do mercado* (Petrópolis, Brazil:Voces, 1989); Franz Hinkelammert, *Sacrificios humanos y sociedad occidental: Lucifer y la Bestia* (San José, Costa Rica: DEI, 1991); Hugo Assmann, *Crítica á logica do exclusão* (São Paulo: Paulus, 1994); Sung, Jung Mo, *Teológia e economia*, 2nd ed. (Petrópolis, Brazil: Vozes, 1995) and *Deus numa economia sem coracao*, 2nd ed. (São Paulo: Paulus, 1994).

Hunger for God, Hunger for Humanity: A Northern Perspective

Heidi Hadsell

Heidi Hadsell, former dean of faculty and vice president of academic affairs at McCormick Theological Seminary, is director of The Ecumenical Institute in Céligny, Switzerland.

The newspaper reports twenty-one, maybe twenty-five, maybe more, unsolved murders over the weekend, basically of poor people in areas of urban poverty, people the city does not claim, did not educate, cannot employ, and does not want; people, especially young men, often of color, who disappear in a slow war of attrition that no one has the stomach to think much about. The same journal reports children mugging children in public places for sports jackets or the hip brand of sports shoes, while adults look on in fear.

Nearby, local and regional authorities attempt the cleanup of a toxic-waste dump that a private company, which left the city, created but did not clean. It took away the jobs, but left the filth and pollution and the costs of cleaning them up. The city can do little. With so many companies leaving and so much unemployment, its tax base has eroded and it is strapped for funds just to provide basic services—with fewer and fewer resources—for more and more people. The rich live in remote communities or in carefully policed pockets in the city. Their party conversation is often about crime and fear and the unfortunate restrictions now placed on children for their own safety—restrictions that not so long ago did not seem necessary.

The pastors of city churches feel under constant siege, using dwindling resources on growing wounds. Their colleagues in richer areas don't really understand and suggest that the struggling inner city churches are an unfortunate drain on resources that could help growing churches elsewhere, often in the suburbs.

Where are we? Well, we are certainly in Chicago. We are also in Rio de Janeiro. We are in New York. We are also in Mexico City. If in former centuries the United States sent missionaries out to spread the gospel in places they found to be very different from their own in culture, economics, and politics, at the end of the twentieth century—in part, because of the mission effort itself—what is most striking in the United States today is not how different we are but how like each other we have become.

If it is indeed the case that commonalities between North and South in the Americas are growing, the mission conversation in the Americas should increasingly be characterized by a common exploration of how to recognize and cope with dynamics and questions that confront both North and South. Such questions will inevitably be economic and political as well as religious. As such conversations take shape, it may well be that despite obvious national and cultural differences, Christian communities in, for example, urban Chicago have more to talk about and share, more in common in terms of life experience, with Christian communities in urban Mexico City than with many communities of Christians in their own suburbs. Similarly, their own understanding of the gospel, their own theology, may well be closer to that of Christians in similar circumstances, members of other denominations both near and far, than to others in their own denomination.

A good model for mission conversations in the future may well be the United Nations conferences and forums in recent years dealing with such themes as the environment, women, child prostitution, and sustainable development. These conferences have enjoyed tremendous international support and appreciation because they have found a way to talk topically that puts everyone under a common umbrella, emphasizing common interests and letting the common issues determine which differences are important in the light of those issues.

For example, the UN conference on women found ways to strengthen and empower all women at the level of moral principle, letting participants in workshops and presentations explore the contextual elements—religious, economic, political—in their own situations, and their similarities and differences in relation to others.

To use another example, the Rio conference on sustainable development was organized around a principle—sustainable development—that was loose enough to be inclusive, thereby making room for many in the conversation, but tight enough to exclude the outer limits. The conversations in Rio were contextual and characterized by a remarkable willingness to talk openly about particular situations, sharing success and failures, developing new strategies and goals together and separately.

Such conversations benefit from their nonofficial nature, since, unlike official UN delegations, no one has unequal power over the other in terms of common decisions to be made or national interests to defend. Rather, different groups bring both different contexts and different insights to the issues, and different resources for dealing with them. This approach assumes a common interest in the issue and rough agreement on the moral principles. It also assumes respect for the other's ability to analyze the specificity of context and the effectiveness of interventions in it. The emphasis is on the sharing of successful strategies, ways in which to strengthen each other, and the search—at least in the first instance—for commonalities and solidarity, not difference.

Existing differences are numerous and important, but in the United States today there is a growing awareness of the extent to which its own political and economic life is currently subject to many of the same dynamics that for many decades American foreign policy, mission efforts, and companies helped to create in other countries across the globe. Thus, for example, the United States looks more and more like Mexico or Brazil or Chile in terms of income distribution patterns than it did just decades ago. Similarly, many big cities and some rural areas in the United States are experiencing high infant mortality rates and illiteracy rates and crises in popular housing, schooling, employment, environment, and infrastructure similar to those of their Southern neighbors.

While it is impossible in a short space to discuss all the trends that together paint a picture of the United States today, it is possible to pinpoint some elements that seem to be of critical importance.

The Shape of the U.S. Economy

Although the United States still enjoys considerable wealth and considerable economic and military power across the globe, the domestic economy has changed shape in recent years in ways that are having a profound effect on U.S. society. The changing shape of the economy has led a number of observers to refer to the "Latin Americanization" of the United States. By this they mean, basically, that increasingly the shape of the U.S. economy looks like that of many countries in Latin America, with a very small percentage of the population owning a very large percentage of the national wealth; with a shrinking middle class, and with the poor growing both more numerous and poorer.

The changes in the shape of the United States economy and society are easily documented and widely reported, although little political discussion is devoted to them. In June 1996, the *New York Times* reported on a study done at the University of Michigan that "the most prosperous 10 percent of American households held 61.1 percent of the nation's wealth in 1989 and 66.8 percent in late 1994. At the same time, the average family in the poorest 10 percent of the nation's population has debts exceeding assets by $7,075 in 1994, measured in 1996 dollars, compared with a negative net worth of $4,744 in 1989."[1]

A Permanent Underclass

Today in the United States there is a substantial underclass at the core of all cities and in a variety of rural areas. It is an underclass that no one wants or needs, no one educates or houses, no one socializes or trains or employs. It is composed of underserved invisible nonvoters and nonconsumers. The economy functions well without them because many millions of others consume and produce.

There seems to be little hope that significant resources or attention will be devoted to them. The *Chicago Tribune* reported with some surprise, "Holy Writ among virtually all economists, politicians and businessmen says that higher productivity will solve all problems. But that hasn't worked here. U.S. productivity has gone up by about 25 percent since 1973, while median wages have fallen—by 22 percent for high school drop-outs, by 7.5 percent for college graduates. Higher productivity should benefit everyone in an economy. These days, it's benefiting capital, not labor, and this will get worse before it gets better."[2]

The "War on Poverty" declared by President Lyndon Johnson in the mid-1960s seems impossible from the perspective of the political and economic climate of the 1990s. Today, most North Americans support the dismantling of government programs designed to aid the poorest and weakest of the population. As the Welfare Reform Act of 1996 goes into effect, cutting dramatically the eligibility and time limits for state support of the poor, it seems clearer and clearer that, while there is no popular enthusiasm for the war on poverty, there is widespread passive support, in the name of a smaller state and lower taxes, for a war on the poor.

The Globalization of the U.S. Economy

Americans still have to come to terms with the fact that today the U.S. economy is global, not only in its ability to impose its economic will on many economies directly through military means, and less directly through international lending institutions and bilateral agreements and the activities of North American companies, but also in the influence that the global economy now has on U.S. economic policies and well-being. While the fact that economies are now global is hardly news to the peoples of many countries whose economic lives have basically been run by the economic and military interests and power of other nations for decades—even centuries—it comes as a shocking surprise to the average American, who faces the new dynamics of global competition with some indignation. In the United States today, cities, regions, and states must compete directly not only with one another, but with countless other cities, regions, and states across the globe in order to attract economic activity. "Since capitalistic economic activity naturally migrates to the places with the fewest regulations and the lowest social charges, national governments are now competing with each other for economic activity much as American states compete with each other to persuade business firms to locate in their state."[3]

U.S. workers, too, must compete in what is increasingly a global arena, often accepting wages and benefits lower than what the U.S. economy and cost of living would suggest, in an attempt to keep jobs from migrating out of the country altogether. In fact, real wages in the United States have been falling for the last several decades, a trend that is often masked in families by the large numbers of women who have entered the work force. Currently, it often takes two salaries to earn in real dollars what two decades ago one salary could earn.

The slowly dawning awareness that the United States is only one player—though still a central player—in global economics, and the awareness that harder work and longer hours often do not guarantee greater pay, generates a lot of popular anger. Frequently this anger is directed against targets that may be easily identifiable but are ultimately not responsible for the white-collar and blue-collar workers' plight. Thus, for example, there is localized anger at multinationals that move out of communities large and small, taking jobs and, in the case of small communities, often destroying those communities' future viability.

At the same time, however, considerable anger has been directed at such targets as legal and illegal immigrants who are perceived to be taking American jobs, and, through access to state aid in various forms of welfare, to be destroying a system that functioned well for several postwar decades. Political discourse in the United States today is focused on gaining favor with a high percentage of voters who support initiatives that are against affirmative action, against immigrants, and against welfare. Apparently the American voter has little tolerance for measures that do not directly benefit himself or herself.

Environmental Issues

Somewhat surprisingly, in a climate that is suspicious—especially of the federal government and the money it spends—there is a degree of consensus in the United States that something must be done to save at least parts of the nation's natural heritage from development and other kinds of environmental destruction. Thus the anger, both social and fiscal, related to the economic insecurity of the American white-collar and blue-collar worker does not extend consistently to environmental issues. Rather, somewhat surprisingly, environmental issues, even when considerable governmental intervention is required, enjoy some popular support, although in opinion polls that support is usually registered as no more than a slim majority. Repeatedly, however, this slim majority has rejected the "either growth and jobs or the environment and unemployment argument" used by many politicians and members of the business community.

With the support of this majority, the Clinton administration has successfully created several new nature reserves and is involved in such attempts as those aimed at saving the Everglades of Florida. Similarly, in many parts of the country and in many cities, efforts at environmental cleanup have been underway, often with the help of federal money, and often with success. These efforts are those of public agencies charged with the cleanup of private waste and environmental destruction that may have gone on for decades. The cleanup efforts are plagued by lack of funds and uneven political support. Still, that support is sufficient to encourage attempts to link environmental matters with other less popular issues such as racism, poverty, and the decay of North American cities.

It is important to note, however, that millions of Americans view virtually any environmental regulation as a full-blown attack on the lifestyle, freedom of choice, and private ownership that they associate with being "American," and they strongly support the ideology of growth and individualism that they have come to view as synonymous with being American. Indeed, on the extreme right there are radical groups, often armed, who distrust and denounce anything the federal government does, environmentally or otherwise, as antithetical to the inalienable property rights of individuals.

Family Issues

While broad social issues, such as racism and growing economic inequality, do not provoke widespread serious debate, the opposite is true of issues closer to home. This debate takes various forms, with a set of issues that are broadly lumped in the category "family values." The focus of the debate is on dynamics that are perceived to be "weakening" the American family, both in its composition and its nature as a moral entity. The debate encompasses various elements: the increase of women in the workforce, abortion, public schools, drugs, and so on. While there is considerable casting of blame, little attention is paid to the influence that changes in the economic structure may have in the development of these dynamics.

The well-documented growing callousness of the American middle class toward the poor and marginal within American society seems to be related to the frequently expressed concern about the health of the American middle-class family. Thus, in an unfortunate and mistaken linkage, the poor and the marginalized, as well as immigrants, all struggling to keep their lives intact and their families together, are held responsible, directly and indirectly, for the strains evident in many middle-class families as both parents work more hours for less pay, children receive mediocre public education, jobs disappear, and cities become more violent and less civil.

Faced with what feels like too many problems of their own, not only do many working-class and middle-class Americans turn their backs on the permanent underclass within their own cities, they also turn their backs on the international arena. In doing so, they follow the same logic of self-interest that they use to evaluate policy choices inside the country. That is, a majority vigorously and noisily objects to any American action abroad that cannot be directly linked to the economic self-interest of the United States.

If the material causes behind these attitudes are generally ignored or misunderstood economic structures and dynamics, often global in scope, the ideological underpinning is the widely shared assumption that there is no limit to human material wants and that humans are inherently and inevitably selfish. At the heart of this apparently clear moral anthropology one finds confusion between what humans *seem* to be—how we act in an ever more competitive, materialistic society—and human nature itself. As a result of such confusion, many among us find it difficult even to imagine other options for self or society.

Since humans are perceived to be primarily competitive and endlessly materialistic, the competitive, unequal, environmentally harmful, materialist economy seems the only suitable system. Thinking is thus trapped inside an unbroken circle of apparently unassailable logic. This logic is well known to those on the receiving end of mission efforts. Many have experienced its assaults, being defined as lazy, lacking in ambition, and irrational because they chose to pursue activities and ends that were not compatible with the logic of the market.

In our reliance on a worldview dominated by the market, we North Americans experience a poverty of the imagination and a depletion of public discourse that, while appealing more and more unabashedly to the selfish parts of our nature, satisfies less and less the yearning for meaning and belonging. We become who we think we are—a people dominated by economic language and images. As a result, somewhat ironically, we lack the vision and language to discuss or comprehend substantive and serious issues, many of which are related to economics, some of which I have mentioned above in both national and global context: the distribution of wealth; the creation of an unwanted, permanent underclass of the excluded; the mutual reinforcement of class, race, and gender in economic and social hierarchies; the environmental disasters we have created but cannot or will not solve; and the unsustainability of a society that cannot inspire vision for, or commitment to, the common good.

Instead, North Americans consume an ever more empty political discourse that is intended to reassure an insecure middle class and placate a growing and ever poorer working class, while it protects the privileges of the really rich. But the substantive issues do not go away and should be grist for the mill of ecumenical conversation in the Americas in the twenty-first century.

Conclusion

If groups from all over the world, both religious and secular, can successfully come together to work and learn, it should be even easier for North and South American Christians, who today not only share many common elements of experience with these issues but also share the biblical mandate to care for the earth as well as the poor, the marginalized, and the outcast. As in the United Nations conferences, the commonalities between North and South American Christians suggest a restructuring of the ecumenical conversation so that debate and controversy, as well as areas of solid agreement, theological conviction, and action may be increasingly horizontal in nature, cutting across nation and denomination and focusing on common interests and issues.

End Notes

1. "Rich Control More of U.S. Wealth, Study Says, as Debts Grow for Poor," *New York Times,* June 22, 1996, p. 17.
2. "New Global Economics Toss the Rule Book out the Door," *Chicago Tribune,* October 20, 1996.
3. Lester Thurow, *The Future of Capitalism,* pp. 129-130.

The Word Became Flesh: Incarnation, Gospel, and Culture in Latin America

Luis N. Rivera-Pagán

Luis N. Rivera-Pagán received his doctorate from
Yale University. He is professor of humanities at
the University of Puerto Rico in Rio Piedras,
and a member of the executive committee of
the Baptist churches of Puerto Rico.

I too sing America, traveling
with the blue pain of the Caribbean sea,
with the oppressed desire of its islands,
the fury of its internal lands.

Let this song ring, not like the vanquished
lethargy of the moribund *quena*
but like a voice that explodes, uniting
the dispersed conscience of the waves.
I too sing a future America [1]

—Rafael Alberti

A Continent in Contradiction

That "future America" sung by Alberti has a history indelibly marked
by the efforts of innumerable men and women living the gospel
under the protection of divine grace and mercy. Unfortunately, that
history is also a procession of bitterness, much of it caused, paradoxically, by those who established themselves as spokespersons of
Christianity. From the first encounter between indigenous American
communities and European Christians in 1492, that contradiction
has marked our history.

Although today's challenges are the priority of those interested in
Latin American and Caribbean cultures, we should not overlook the
history of human endeavors, lest we risk falling into lightweight,
superficial formulas. The effort to overcome what the literary critic

Arcadio Díaz Quiñones has called "the policy of forgetfulness" of "a history full of silences and concealment,"[2] has become transformed into the urgent labor of a constellation of grassroots and intellectual organizations that undertake social efforts. As José Lezama Lima writes in his great novel-poem, *Paradiso*, creative sensibility is composed of two concurrent efforts: on the one hand, the search for the unknown future and "its creative elements that are yet to be configured," and, on the other, "the revival of the past, the mysterious decision to embark on the incunabula."[3] The memory of the origin of those to whom we refer belongs to indigenous communities and African American peoples.

Our friend and colleague Jung Mo Sung, in his excellent presentation "Hunger for God, Hunger for Bread, Hunger for Humanity,"[4] has placed before us the challenges raised by the slow-paced free-market globalization of capitalism and its culture of insensitivity. That lack of sensitivity is demonstrated not only, as he indicated, by deafness to cries of "hunger for bread" but also by myopia in the face of the "hunger for God" and "hunger for humanity" that express the very particular spirituality and religious sensibility of subjugated and despised peoples.[5] The themes of culture and spirituality, therefore, take on renewed force for those who aspire to make incarnate the gospel as evidence that the Word became flesh.[6]

On the eve of the new millennium, I would like to point out some challenges raised by this theme concerning people of the Americas whose cultures have been disdained and undervalued. These observations are made in a time that suffers a "messianic drought," in Elsa Tamez's[7] suggestive phrase, but that, paradoxically and simultaneously, is the prelude—as José Duque[8] has pointed out—of a new *kairos*, manifesting the obstinacy and tenacity of hope.[9]

From Hatuey to Túpac Amaru: The Way of the Cross for Indigenous Communities

Traditionally, Protestant churches and theologians have described the founding events of the discovery, conquest, and Christianizing of the Americas in a somber manner. Certainly there is much to criticize and condemn in that enterprise, as can be easily confirmed by reading the prophetic denouncements of Bartolomé de Las Casas, who, as an Iberian Catholic of the sixteenth century, had little sympathy for Lutherans and Calvinists.[10] Nevertheless, the very name de Las Casas is a reminder that those events were never exempt from debate and dispute. Perhaps it is true, as some scholars have affirmed, that no empire has had its legitimacy disputed with such vigor as that of Spain in the sixteenth century.

A good part of this debate revolved around the legality of military and political conquest (cf. the Dominican theologian Francisco de Vitoria's famous conference about the illegitimate and legitimate titles that were wielded to claim, through war, the sovereignty that he recognized, in principle, as belonging to the native princes).[11] Nevertheless, an acute and merciless theological controversy about the evangelization of Americans was provoked, dealing mainly with three crucial points:[12] the value of indigenous cultures, the validity of their forms of worship, and the use of force as a missionary strategy.

Christianity and Indigenous Cultures

Does the Christianizing of indigenous American peoples imply the drastic and total transformation of their habits of social existence? The most interesting thing by far is not that a considerable number of European theologians, jurists, and officials denied all symbolic value in the cultures of the original peoples of the Americas. This was to be expected. Furthermore, the renewal of Hellenic political philosophy provided the concept of the "barbarian" or "savage" in its Aristotelian variant, attributing to it the condition of "natural servitude"[13]—broadened to denote a double inferiority—of culture and religion. Rather, it is extraordinary that there were *any* Spanish theologians who resisted ethnocentrism and proclaimed the value of indigenous cultures.

In the polyphony of sixteenth-century voices, there is the dissident exclamation, the counterpoint, of de Las Casas, who wrote work after work—treatises, histories, chronicles, memorials, epistles, denouncements, sermons, confessional procedures, even his last will and testament—attempting to demonstrate a central thesis: the human wholeness, integral rationality, and free will of native Americans. For the Dominican friar, "all the nations of the world are men."[14] To demonstrate this thesis, he wrote the monumental work *Apologética historia sumaria,* the most impressive effort of a white, European Christian seeking to demonstrate the integral rationality and human completeness of non-European, nonwhite, non-Christian peoples. The entire objective of that extraordinary work was to give evidence of the multiple ways in which "[all] the nations of the world are men, and of all men; and each is one more definition . . .

all have their understanding and their will; and their free will as they are formed in the image and likeness of God."[15]

As can be inferred by these references, the debate about the value of the symbolic and imaginary cultural worlds of the original peoples leads to the crucial question that, for the first time, like "a voice crying in the wilderness," would be uttered by the Dominican preacher Antonio de Montesinos: "Are these not men? Do they not have rational souls?" The controversy about cultures was transformed from the first moment into a polemic about the humanity of the inhabitants of these lands. Undoubtedly, this relates to the modern question of human rights, but also, and above all, to the evangelical and prophetic obligation to relate to indigenous peoples within the horizon of justice and divine mercy.[16] For this reason Montesinos asks his next question: "Are you not compelled to love them as yourselves?"[17]

The Value of the Religious Expression of Indigenous Peoples

Are indigenous forms of worship "seeds of the Word," "preparation for the Gospel," or, rather, "diabolical mimesis"? Can the culture of indigenous peoples be vigorously and creatively preserved if their forms of worship are scorned or eradicated? Again, authority was in the hands of the extensive group of theologians and members of the ecclesial hierarchy who dismissed all native religious expression as "idolatry"—to be absolutely rooted out, according to Old Testament norms.[18] How do we preserve culture and simultaneously unravel it from a form of worship considered diabolical? This dilemma becomes an insoluble enigma for theologians, missionaries, and educators who are at the same time perplexed, fascinated, and terrified when confronted by the traditions, rites, and ceremonies of newly discovered peoples who have been inserted into European Christians' horizon of power and knowledge. Concerning the campaigns of the sixteenth and seventeenth centuries in Peru to eradicate the prevailing "idolatries," Pierre Duviols asserts, *"C'est la culture indigène tout entière qui risque de tomber sous la coup de l'interdit."*[19] [The entire indigenous culture is completely in danger of falling under the interdict.] The collective trauma implied by that threat is difficult to imagine. And from the contradictory effort to save some souls by freeing them from forms of worship that were part of their culture, the perpetual paradox that is Latin America was traumatically born.

Again, a prophetic voice was sounded with vigor. In his *Comentarios reales,* Inca Garcilaso de la Vega has designed an alternative perspective, a dissident counterpoint. Conscious of the contempt that the great pre-Columbian cultures suffered at the hands of Hispanic chroniclers and intellectuals, Garcilaso has defended the idea that Incan religion was a positive development, because it led to 1) the predominance among Andean natives of natural law or human rational sociability and 2) the overcoming of animistic idolatry in the direction of monotheism—first solar and then spiritual—by its reverence for Pachacamac, the transcendental animator of all being.

In Incan worship prior to the arrival of European missionaries, there existed the fertile seed of a notion of a universal and spiritual deity. Garcilaso has reproduced a legend according to which one of the last Incas, Hayna Cápac, intuited that the sun was only a celestial body under the sovereignty of a superior deity. King Huana Cápac then said, "This Our Father Sun must have another greater Lord more powerful than he, who orders him to take this road which he must ceaselessly take everyday."[20]

It is a bold attempt at historical reconstruction that seeks to place the Incan empire in a position similar to that which the Church Fathers held in Greco-Latin antiquity. The primacy in the process of civilizing indigenous peoples and inculcating them with a monotheistic and spiritual vision of divinity competes, in this heterodox vision, with indigenous protagonists, not with Spanish conquerors. In this manner, from within mixed Ibero-American Christianity, indigenous forms of worship are refuted as satanic idolatries and are seen as "evangelical preparation." Thus, the principal patristic tradition of dealing with the Gentile world is recovered—a tradition initiated by St. Justin Martyr and culminating with St. Augustine.

Evangelizing Conquest or Missionary Action

Should evangelization be preceded by military conquest or, on the contrary, should it have nothing to do with military effort? Is the peaceful Christianizing of indigenous communities possible? The greater number of questioners—from Fray Ramón Pané[21] at the end of the fifteenth century to José de Acosta,[22] a century later—understood that the evangelizing of indigenous communities could not be assured without a high degree of military violence. That strategy or missionary theology could be described as *evangelizing conquest.*

Nevertheless, beginning with the Dominican friars of Hispaniola at the beginning of the sixteenth century, a different and opposite missionary theology was outlined. It was a theology that could be called a mission of action, founded exclusively on peaceful persuasion. It was first recommended by Fray Pedro de Córdoba, leader of the religious community at Hispaniola, who suggested to the young King Carlos that the first approach to indigenous peoples should be exclusively religious, without the company of armed men. This suggestion grew, on the one hand, out of the tragic experience of the people of the Antilles, "because these islands and newly-discovered and found lands, filled with people . . . are, and today have been, destroyed and depopulated by the great cruelties that have been committed in them by Christians." He drew a biblical analogy to express the oppression to which native peoples were submitted: "Not even Pharaoh and the Egyptians committed as much cruelty against the people of Israel." There was also a dissident vision—as an alternative to the initial expression of a utopia—that reappeared continuously throughout the sixteenth century. It was the possibility of reconstructing in the New World, free from European decadence, the virtues of apostolic Christianity. "If only preachers came among them [these ill-fated Christians] without force and violence, I feel that it would be possible to establish in these lands a church almost as excellent as the primitive [early] church."[23]

The Dominicans on Hispaniola insisted that missionary efforts should proceed without violent coercion or forced servitude: "People from the New World that God gave to Your Majesty can be brought to God, to the soft yoke of Christ and his faith . . . without having to take their things by force, and conserving their titles, except for the supreme jurisdiction that belongs to Your Majesty . . . and not swiftly as is done now until they are killed." In the event that the crown and its advisers would not consider the evangelizing of indigenous peoples as feasible without the intervention of warlike actions, the friars proposed a radical measure that was not accepted, namely, that indigenous peoples were to remain undisturbed in their infidelity and isolation: "If . . . you consider that this is impossible, . . . from now we entreat Your Majesty, for the good that we want for your royal conscience and soul, that it is better, Your Majesty, if you order that they be undisturbed, since it is better that they go to hell on their own, rather than us and them, and the name of Christ be blasphemed among those peoples as a result of the poor example of our [people] and that Your Majesty's soul, which is worth more than the entire world, suffer harm."[24]

According to this prophetic and evangelical focus, liberty and life are preferable to servitude and death, although these may be sacrilegiously masked with the name of the Crucified.[25]

Perhaps at no other time in history did theological polemics acquire greater political and social currency. The three points in debate—the value of indigenous cultures, the validity of their forms of worship, and the use of military force as a missionary strategy shook the minds and hearts of the principal Spanish theologians of the time and drastically touched the roots of native American communities. These are not footnotes in the history of our peoples that are of interest only to the erudite. These were decisive elements in the formation of colonial Christianizing, in its baroque flourishing, and finally in its collapse.[26] They are still relevant since they point to the nucleus of what we must consider today on the eve of Christianity's third millennium, the relationship between the perennial themes of incarnation and *kenosis*, the cultures of the peoples and the theologies in which they attempt to manifest their distinctive worldviews, and their sensibilities regarding the sacred and transcendental. All of this, in the special contexts of our own day—as in the sixteenth century—plays itself out in the midst of violent and dehumanizing structures. Certainly, these are political and social controversies, but they are also eminently theological questions that present a challenge to the understanding and practice of faith. They revolve, above all, around the subjects that interest us in this session: What is the significance of the Word becoming flesh? What is the just relationship between the gospel of the Word becoming incarnate and the cultures of our peoples?

From this tortuous polemic emerges, in addition, the utopia of the church in solidarity with the poor and humble of the earth. It is described in "lucid hallucination" by the elderly Bartolomé de Las Casas, his soul heavy with fatigue and bitterness but with the old tenacity, in his last epistle to Pope Pius V,[27] in which he announces—against the grain of contemporary hegemonies—the birth of a poor church that restores the goods produced by the sweat and blood of the oppressed, that knows and respects the language of the people, that identifies with their cultures, that is humbled with the despised, and that, in the final analysis—being indispensable—is absolutely committed to offer its life as an oblation to the persecuted.

The Return of Quetzalcoatl

From that tradition of utopia in the prophetic church, a new interest in rethinking the understanding and practice of faith from the perspective of indigenous American communities has flourished.[28] For lack of time, we can point only briefly to significant contributions that have been made to general theological reflection as a result of this effort. It is a key indigenous theological and ecclesial task, but it also demands the attention of all those interested in the future of our peoples and their spirituality.

- *The land.* The theme of the land as divine gift and mother of the community is crucial in every theological dialogue with the original peoples of the Americas. It is natural that it should be thus, since the land was one of the first things of which they were stripped. Furthermore, this theme serves as a reminder of the centrality of the promise of the land in Hebrew-Christian Scriptures, from the divine covenant with Abraham (Genesis 12:1) to the eschatological vision of the new Jerusalem (Revelation 21:10). Undoubtedly, as pointed out by Leonardo Boff in recent years, this theme is related to the current interest in themes of nature and the overcoming of Western anthropocentrism.[29]

- *The community.* Western symbolic imagery agonizes over the concept of individuality as distinct from the community as the matrix of the person. Even when individuality was recognized, at least rhetorically, as a universal attribute, Illuminism took the premise that enlightened individuals had the means for liberation from ideologies that seek to destroy autonomy.[30] The value of this position—in the midst of the current postmodern criticisms—is undeniable. Nevertheless, the spiritual rupture that provokes division between individual and community is also undeniable and requires us to pay attention to the communal spirituality of peoples who have resisted the individualistic alienation that afflicts the West—an alienation that led Camus to assert in an heroic tone that "there is only one really serious philosophical question: suicide."[31]

- *Rites, ceremonies and myths.* Traditional ecumenical discussion has taken place among the different Christian churches, above all among those that adhere to shared doctrines formulated in the four initial councils (Nicea, Constantinople, Ephesus, and Chalcedon). Nevertheless, indigenous communities, in a manner similar to African American peoples, have demanded respect and recognition of the religious expressions gathered in their myths, ceremonies, and rites. Interreligious dialogue is being superimposed on traditional ecumenism and there is a new tolerance of alternative spirituality.[32]

- *The feast of community.* Life for indigenous peoples is difficult and, on occasion, borders on misery. Bartolomé de Las Casas called them "the poorest of the poor," a condition that has not changed in many places throughout the Americas. Yet, during significant times the community gathers to celebrates its existence. Rigoberta Menchú, who carries on her shoulders a history of pain and suffering, nevertheless dedicates a good part of her autobiography to descriptions of celebrations by her people as expressions of joy and gratitude for life, and of solidarity in the midst of suffering.[33] Perhaps our congregations can learn something from this tradition of the feast as a celebration of life, and thus rescue our amusements from the banality into which they have fallen.

- *Sacred duality.* The establishment of Western patriarchy has been the object of much study and even greater criticism.[34] Without adopting romantic positions that distort the history of indigenous communities, it may yet be accurate to suggest that in them a dual conception of divinity predominates—a concept that can contribute to overcoming Western androcentrism and misogyny. The feminine face of God is shown incarnate in the original peoples, those who nursed the infancy of our American homelands. It could be asserted that the worship of Mary in Latin America and the Caribbean is built to a great extent on previous indigenous worship to mother goddesses. This has been fruitfully studied in relation to the Virgin of Guadalupe/Tonactinzin, in Mexico, and the Virgin de la Caridad del Cobre/Atabey, in Cuba.[35]

From Saint James to Ogún Fai: Theological Challenges of African American Peoples

Compared with the considerable number of theological essays about indigenous communities, little has been written about African American communities.[36] That is surprising, since work about the diaspora of African peoples and their exuberant spiritual life in the territories of the New World is wide-ranging and excellent. Among the existing reflections, several significant themes emerge for a theology that moves in the direction of Word and gospel incarnate.

- *The diaspora.* As the land is a significant thematic axis for indigenous communities, for African American communities it is uprootedness and forced exile. African peoples were violently removed from their native communities and taken to strange lands in unknown and foreign ecosystems.[37] They are peoples of the diaspora, compelled to reconstruct their spiritual world on foreign soil and under different skies. The biblical theme of the diaspora acquires renewed force in this context.[38]

- *The captivity.* Slavery is a crucial historical axis for the consciousness of African American peoples. The exceptional theological and legal debate about servitude and slavery in the sixteenth century concerned itself with aboriginal communities. Meanwhile, America was being filled with African faces and bodies forced to endure fierce slavery. At the peak of the trade in Africans and of their introduction into Brazil, the Jesuit Antonio Vieira summed up from the pulpit slavery's prevailing theological justification: "Your captivity is not a misfortune, but rather a great miracle, because your fathers will be in hell for all eternity, while you will be saved, thanks to slavery."[39]

- *Noah's curse.* Whereas aboriginal ethnic groups are predominantly defined by cultural rather than biological categories, in African American communities negritude has been imposed as a sign of social inferiority. That which is black is degraded and scorned, and it seems impossible to escape from that stigma. The beautiful ebony skin becomes a prison for bodies and souls from which one can become liberated only after a long struggle against scorn and low self-esteem. Negritude becomes identified with slavery and is legitimized with Noah's curse of his son Ham (Genesis 9:18-27).[40]

- *Syncretism.* Recent research into forms of religious expression of African American peoples has revealed an exceptional strategy of the celebration of Carnival through which their distinctive spiritual sensibility learns to survive in hostile situations. Their religion is a cultural mix unlike that of indigenous communities and one that, consequently, presents different challenges to those seeking a new understanding and practice of the gospel. Carnival, which in Latin America attains its splendor in black communities, is transmuted into a jubilant metaphor of this distinctive syncretism.[41]

- *Music.* There is no way to respect the culture of African American communities without recognizing the enormous vitality of their historical memory, reflected not so much in mythical narratives, as among indigenous peoples, but, rather, in music. It is through rhythm and rhyme that black people express grief and sadness as well as their enormous capacity for resistance and hope. In his first novel, *Ecué-Yamba-Ó! Historia afrocubana* (1927) Alejo Carpentier perceived the vital centrality of music, especially the use of drums, to the expression and preservation of African Antillean spirituality.[42]

These themes are of primary theological interest not only to African Americans but also to those interested in discovering hermeneutic keys for the renewal of ecclesiastical thought at the dawn of the new millennium. [43] They provoke crucial challenges for the incarnation of the gospel in the history of the peoples whose cultural identity has been subjugated and despised. They contain anguish and hope, as expressed in a Creole song that Carpentier has included in another of his novels:

> Yenvalo moin Papa!
> Moin pas mangé q'm bambó
> Yenvalou, Papá, yanvalou moin!
> Ou vlai moin lavé chaudier,
> Yenvalo Moin?"

> [Will I have to continue washing pots?
> Will I have to continue eating bamboo?
> Oh, father, my father
> suffering is such a long, long time!][44]

Postlude: The Renaissance of Utopia

The Peruvian writer José María Arguedas[45] and the Cuban, Alejo Carpentier,[46] recognized several decades ago the significance of the claims made by indigenous and African American peoples. On the one hand, those claims seek to reconstruct the concept of nationhood in a way that includes the polyphony—not always symphonic—of ethnic groups, cultures, spiritualities, languages, and forms of religions expression, freed of imposed uniformity. On the other hand, the work of these men points to a possible new theological reading of American cultural history, to a reconceptualizing of the understanding and practice of faith, in which—thanks to a surprising eruption of the Spirit—the plural dialogue of Pentecost is reenacted[47] and new paths are designed for the inculturation of the gospel.[48]

It is significant that the narrative portion of Arguedas' last novel, *El zorro de arriba y el zorro de abajo* (1971), culminates with a reading by a priest, Father Cardozo, of I Corinthians 13, Paul's poem about love, and a meditation about the implications of this text for current Peruvian social and cultural conflicts. The anxious autobiographical sections of this painful work conclude with a strange soliloquy, in great measure directed to "Gustavo [Gutierrez], the theologian of the liberating God," about the enormously significant consequences of the struggle between the God of the powerful and the Liberator, "He who becomes reintegrated."[49] For his part, Carpentier concludes one of his last narratives, *Concierto barroco* (1974), with a concert by Louis Armstrong, in which he makes the narrator exclaim: "The Bible once again became rhythm and dwelt among us.[50] The sacred rhythm, nurtured by the prayers and supplications of suffering, subjugated black people, is transmuted in this delicious tale with the announcement of a new incarnation of the Word.[51]

This is not something unprecedented in our history. José Lezama Lima, the brilliant Cuban writer, has affirmed in open challenge to traditional didactic schema that the essential elements of Latin American baroque art of the eighteenth century do not rest solely on European paradigms but, rather, on the peculiar synthesis of a mixture incorporating that which is European (Hispanic), autochthonous (indigenous), and black (African). It is an exceptional mixture, drawing on symbols and artistic images from a variety of origins that seek to shape the destiny of our peoples in clearly cultural religious creations.[52]

Laós and *Éthnos*: The Paulist Revolution

The Greek word éthnos does not have a good history. During the golden age of Athenian philosophy it acquired a pejorative meaning, referring to those beyond the pale of Hellenic language and culture, coming closer, semantically, to the term *bárbaros* (barbarian). In the Septuagint, a key antagonistic disjunction is found between the "people" (*laós*) of God and the "pagan or Gentile nations" (*éthnê*). Although God is the creator of all nations (*éthnê*), God grants Israel the exclusive distinction of being God's people (*laós*). Hellenic Judaism proselytized with intensity but conserved and identified the difference between *laós* and *ethnê*. Converts had to adopt the worship and cultural traditions of Israel; Gentile nations were relegated to eternal condemnation.[53]

In this context, the last words of Paul in the Acts of the Apostles carry with them a Copernican revolution in the biblical concept of divine providence: "Let it be known to you then that this salvation of God (*tò sôtêrion toû theoû*) has been sent to the Gentiles (*toîs éthnesin*); they will listen" (Acts 28: 28). God's grace is proclaimed to the *éthnê*, and the ethnic groups. All ethnic groups are given the possibility of becoming integrated into the people of God, leaving aside all forms of discrimination and all prejudicial forms of worship and culture that have tried to claim the privilege of divine providence. It is evident that in the book of Acts, *éthnos* and *éthnê* have a meaning that is not limited to the racial; they include what we today call—in very broad terms—culture.

The concepts and missionary practices of Christianity have, nonetheless, had the periodic effect of reconstructing the distinction between God's *laós* and the *éthnê*, identifying the first with Western, white, and Northern, and the second with non-Western, dark, and Southern cultures. The multiethnic and pluricultural opening that Paul gives to the gospel acquires great pertinence in that indigenous communities and African American peoples demand full respect and dignity for their cultures. As heirs and heiresses of that history, we need to pay special attention to the words with which Paul concludes his radical transformation of the biblical message: "This salvation has been sent to the ethnic groups; they will listen."

This theological perspective necessarily assumes the negation of one's own traditions: from the bosom of Western Christianity, Bartolomé de Las Casas extracts the ironic unmasking word and makes it incarnate by imparting authentic continuity to the prophetic lineage. This certainly implies leaving aside the traditional separation between "civilized peoples," with their prerogatives and privileges of dominance, and "backward peoples," destined for submission to the free will of the former—what the Palestinian-American scholar Edward Said has called "the fundamental ontological distinction between the West and the rest of the world."[54] Likewise, it assumes overcoming—in the right and in fact; in personal subjectivity and in social objectivity—the painful current reality identified by Gustavo Gutierrez: "Today indigenous peoples and most of the black population in this continent continue to see their ways of living, values, customs, their right to life and liberty trampled."[55]

In the relationship between human cultures and Christian faith, all peoples have their own particular contribution—that which marks and distinguishes them as historically unique. However, a sinister threat to peoples' identities has frequently been hidden under the banner of the universality of faith and the unity of the church. Today there are signs that on the eve of a new millennium, the era of cultural and theological redress for pluriform faith communities—men and women of the corn as well as the drum—has finally come. From this we will all leave enriched.

Earlier I alluded to the utopia of the church in solidarity, set forth by Bartolomé de Las Casas at the end of his long and troubled life in a letter to Pope Pius V. It is a church in which the subjugated and scorned have a privileged place at the supper table, in which those who have been excluded become the preferred. As do all human utopias, this one, founded on the most precious traditions of Christian memory, suffers from the implacable erosion into disillusionment and frustration that characterizes all human history. Miraculously, however, that history is also perennially fresh and new. Allow me to quote some verses of rebelliousness and illusion by the great Nicaraguan poet Rubén Darío, who exclaims in the midst of this end-of-the-century pessimism and resignation:

> I have launched my cry amongst you swans
> who have been faithful in disillusionment. . . .
> Oh! lands of the sun and harmony,
> yet you keep the hope of Pandora's box." [56]

End Notes

1. Rafael Alberti, "Yo también canto a América", *El poeta en la calle* (Madrid: Ediciones Aguilar, 1978), p. 91.

2. Arcadio Díaz Quiñonez, *La memoria rota: Ensayos sobre cultura y política* (Río Piedras, Puerto Rico: Ediciones Huracán, 1993).

3. José Lezama Lima, *Paradiso* (Madrid: Cátedra, 1993), pp. 498-499. Lezama uses the Latin word *incunabula*, which refers to origins, infancy.

4 Jung Mo Sung, "Fome de Deus, fome de pão, fome de humanidade," in the Missiology Consultation, "Discerning God's Mission: Hope and Justice for All in the Americas" (San José, Costa Rica: sponsored by the National Council of the Churches of Christ in the USA, April 21-25, 1997). Also consult his doctoral dissertation in *Teologia e economia: Repensando a teologia da libertacao e utopias* (Petrópolis, Brazil: Vozes, 1994).

5.Ibid.

6. Corrective steps are being taken in Latin American theological circles to confront old themes of popular culture and religious expression, as shown in several essays in the report of the Latin American and Caribbean Ecumenical Theological Education Community's (CETELA) fourth theological session. José Duque, ed., *Por una sociedad donde quepan todos: Teología de Abya-Yala en los albores del siglo xxi* (San José, Costa Rica: Comunidad de Educación Teológica Ecuménica Latinoamericana-Caribeña/Departamento Ecuménico de Investigaciones, 1996).

7. Elsa Tamez, "Cuando los horizontes se cierran: Una reflexión sobre la razón utópica de Qohélet," *Cristianismo y sociedad,* año 33, núm. 123, 1995, p. 7.

8. José Duque, "El espíritu protestante en el quehacer de la Teología de la Liberación," *Por una sociedad donde quepan todos,* p.121.

9. Among the many works that manifest this obstinacy and tenacity of hope, Pablo Freire's *Pedagogia de la esperanza: Un reencuentro con la pedagogia del oprimido* (México, D.F.: Siglo XXI, 1993) stands out. The great educator reviews his life and work and places them in the whirlwinds that have shaken Latin America during the second half of the twentieth century.

10. A great many works have been written about Las Casas and his extraordinary prophetic, historiographic, theological, and ecclesial efforts to assert that relations between European Christians and original peoples of the Americas be conducted according to divine justice and the gospel. Among these: Luis N.Rivera-Pagán, *A Violent Evangelism: The Political and Religious Conquest of the Americas* (Louisville: Westminster-John Knox Press, 1992), and Gustavo Gutiérrez, *Las Casas: In Search of the Poor of Jesus Christ* (Maryknoll, N.Y.: Orbis Books, 1993). This work is the culmination of three decades of Gutierrez's reflections on the history of prophetic and liberating theology in Latin America.

11. *Obras de Francisco de Vitoria: Relecciones teológicas.* A critical edition of the Latin text, Spanish version, general introduction, and introductions with the study of his theological-legal doctrine, ed. Teófilo Urdanoz, O.P. (Madrid: Biblioteca de Autores Cristianos, 1960).

12. I have developed this issue to a greater extent in my essay, "La evangelización de los pueblos americanos: Algunas reflexiones históricas," in *Etnias, culturas y teologías,* ed. Manuel Quintero (Quito, Ecuador: Consejo Latinoamericano de Iglesias, 1996), pp. 25-57.

13. Among the many examples only one is necessary: One of the writers of the "leyes de Burgos" [Laws of Burgos] (December 1512), the university graduate Gregorio, states that, according to Aristotle's categories, indigenous peoples are "slaves and barbarians . . . that, according to all, are like animals who speak." Quoted by Bartolomé de las Casas, in *Historia de las Indias* (Mexico, D.F.: Fondo de Cultura Económica, 1986), 1.3, c. 12, t. 2, p. 472.

14. Ibid., 1. 2, c. 58, t. 2, p. 396.

15. *Apologética historia sumaria,* ed. Edmundo O'Gorman, 2 vols. (México, D.F.: Universidad Nacional Autónoma, 1967), 1.3, c. 48, t.1, pp. 257-258.

16. The military dictatorships in power during the quarter century between 1964 and 1989 taught us the essential nature of respect for civil and basic human rights, many times despised by the radical left, who paid an extreme price for that disdain. Nevertheless, Latin American liberation theology is correct when it emphasizes, as its own contribution to Christian conscience rooted in prophetic and evangelical biblical texts, the rights of the poor, excluded, and dispossessed. Cf. Luis N. Rivera-Pagán, "Los sueños del ciervo: Justicia y esperanza solidaria," *Cristianismo y sociedad,* año 33, núm. 123, 1995, pp. 33-35.

17. Montesinos's sermon is known thanks to Bartolomé de Las Casas, who copied it in his *Historia de las Indias,* 1. 3, c. 4, t. 2, pp.441-442.

18. Cf. for Andean forms of worship, Pierre Duviols, *La lutte contre les religions autochtones dans le Pérou colonial: L'extirpation de l'idolatrie entre 1532 at 1660* (París: Institut Français d'Études Andines, 1971) and for that of Mesoamerica, Robert Ricard, *La conquista espiritual de México: Ensayo sobre el apostolado y los métodos misioneros de las órdenes mendicantes en la Nueva España de 1523 a 1572* (México, D.F.: Fondo de Cultura Económica, 1986). Duviols wrote that "demonology was undoubtedly the theological science most common among conquerors and colonizers," (Op.cit., p.29).

19. Ibid., p. 240.

20. Inca Garcilaso de la Vega, *Comentarios reales,* 2 vols. (México, D.F.: Secretaría de Educación Pública - Universidad National Autónoma, 1982), vol. 2, IX 10, p. 338. This work has been accused of self-interested reconstruction of the past, but it is a criticism

that to a greater or lesser extent is valid for all the histories written during the sixteenth and seventeenth centuries about the rise of Latin America. Hence, Edmundo O'Gorman's excellent expression, "the invention of America." The central point rests in the classic Ciceronian phrase: cui bono? For the benefit of whom, and from whose perspective is it written?

21. *Relación acerca de las antigüedades de los indios,* José Juan Arrom, ed. (México, D.F.: Siglo XXI, 1987).

22. *De procuranda indorum salute (Predicación del evangelio en las Indias,* 1588), ed. Francisco Mateos, S.J. (Madrid: Colección España Misionera, 1952).

23. *Colección de documentos inéditos relativos al descubrimiento, conquista y organización de las antiguas posesiones españolas de América y Oceanía, sacados de los Archivos del Reino y muy especialmente del de India,* (Joaquín Pacheco, Francisco Cárdenas, and Luis Torres de Mendoza, eds., 42 vols. (Madrid: Imp. De Quirós, 1864-1884), vol. 11, pp. 217-218. The missive is from 28 May 1517.

24. Ibid., vol. 11, pp.243-249.

25. The position assumed by Dominicans on Hispaniola will culminate in the voluminous treatise of Bartolomé de Las Casas, *Del único modo de atraer a todos los pueblos a la verdadera religión.* By means of an extensive theoretical treatment about the intrinsic relationship between Christian faith, liberty, and the preaching of peace, full of biblical, patrician, canonical, and philosophical references, Las Casas reiterates that conversion is genuine only if it is deprived of all coercion, if it is achieved through "persuasion of the intellect by means of reason, and the invitation and gentle divine inspiration of the will." *Del único modo de atraer a todos los pueblos a la verdadera religión* (México, D.F.: Fondo de Cultura Económica, 1942), p. 7. There is an English translation: *The Only One Way,* ed. Helen Rand Parish, trans. F. Sullivan (New York: Paulist Press, 1992).

26. For the development of colonial Christianizing, see Luis N. Rivera-Pagán, *Entre el oro y la fe: El dilema de América* (Río Piedras, Puerto Rico: Editorial de la Universidad de Puerto Rico, 1995). For its baroque flourishing, see José Lezama Lima's beautiful book, *La expresión americana* (La Habana: Editorial Letras Cubanas, 1993, first published 1957). For its collapse, see Gabriel García Márquez, *Of Love and Other Demons* (New York: Knopf, 1995). I have assayed a historical-theological reading of this novel in "Sierva María de Todos los Angeles. El amor y la virgen endemoniada en Gabriel García Márquez," *Vida y pensamiento* (Seminario Bíblico Latinoamericano), vol. 16, núm. 1, pp. 84-115.

27. It is copied in *Fray Bartolomé de Las Casas: Doctrina,* ed. Agustín Yáñez (México, D.F.: Universidad Nacional Autónoma, 1941), pp. 163-165. This letter bears an audacious violation of royal authority by communicating directly with the Pope without passing through the channel of the Castillian Council of the Indies, a mechanism of state control, which up until that time Las Casas had obeyed. It is a demand to reconstruct the historical function of the American Church by placing the Church –without ambivalence or ambiguity— on the path of liberation. Therefore, in a nutshell, the missive contains a new and challenging ecclesiology.

28. Cf. Paulo Suess, *La nueva evangelización: Desafíos históricos y pautas culturales* (Quito: Ediciones ABYA-YALA, 1993); Paulo Suess (organizador), *Culturas y evangelización: La unidad de la razón evangélica en la multiplicidad de sus voces* (Quito: Ediciones ABYA-YALA, 1992); Paulo Suess, *Evangelizar desde los proyectos históricos de los otros: Diez ensayos de misionología* (Quito: Ediciones ABYA-YALA, 1995); Manuel Marzal et al., *The Indian Face of God in Latin America* (Maryknoll, N.Y. Orbis Books, 1996); and *Búsqueda de Espacios para la vida: Primer encuentro continental de teologías afro, indígena y cristiana* (Cayambe, Ecuador, 1994); and from several authors, *Los pueblos de la esperanza* (Quito: Ediciones ABYA-YALA/Consejo Latinoamericano de Iglesias, 1996).

29. Leonardo Boff, *Ecology and Liberation: The Emergence of a New Paradigm* (Maryknoll, N.Y.: Orbis Books, 1995).

30. Cf. Bernardo Campos, "Educación cristiana y cultura andina," in *Por una sociedad que quepan todos,* ed. José Duque, pp. 318-321.

31. Albert Camus, *El mito de Sísifo* (Buenos Aires: Editorial Losada, 1975), p. 13.

32. See the presentation of José Míguez Bonino, "Hacia un ecumenismo del espíritu," presented in January 1995 in the third general assembly of the Latin American Council of Churches, and the reaction of the Brazilian theologian Nancy Cardoso Pereira, "Ecumenismo e pluralidade religiosa," in *Renacer a la esperanza* (Quito: Consejo Latinoamericano de Iglesias, 1995), pp. 31-38 and 147-150. Cardoso Pereira challenges traditional ecumenism in terms that stirred debate in the meeting: "I feel that any reflection on the topic departs from a challenge: there is not only one God, there is not only one Lord, Jesus Christ and there is not only one people of God. Only a short time ago, we were learning to co-exist with plural religious experiences that were outside the fundamental premises of Christianity and we tried to become accustomed to Latin American reality and the many gods and goddesses . . . and the many redeeming mediations; and the various forms of understanding as a people the relationship with that which is sacred" (p. 147). Manuel Quintero has indicated, with reason, that religious pluralism is increasingly an essential sign of all Latin America. He points to the growth of Pentecostalism, the revitalization of ethnic religions (Indian American and African American), and the height of what has become known as "the new religious movements." "Oikoumene: Venturas y desventuras en la antesala del tercer milenio," *Cristianismo y sociedad*, vol. 33, num. 124, 1995 pp. 43-58. Cf. Carlos Duarte, *Las mil y una caras de la religión: Sectas y nuevos movimientos religosos en América Latina* (Quito, Ecuador: CLAI, 1995). Walter Altmann, in his written intervention, "The Challenge to Ecumenism and Mission in the Face of Increasing Religious Pluralism in Latin America," for the Missiology Consultation, skillfully emphasizes the opportunities and dangers that increasing pluralism presents to the main Christian confessions and the ecumenical movement.

33. Rigoberta Menchú and Elizabeth Burgos, *Me llamo Rigoberta Menchú y así me nació la conciencia* (México, D.F.: Siglo XXI, décima edición, 1994).

34. Cf. Gerda Lerner, *The Creation of Patriarchy* (New York: Oxford University Press, 1986).

35. This last point reflects a mixture that is more complex than the first since it appears also to involve the Yoruba feminine deity Oshun. See Antonio Benítez-Rojo, *The Repeating Island: The Caribbean and the Postmodern Perspective* (Durham, N.C.: Duke University Press, 1992), pp. 12-16, 52-53.

36. See *Cultura negra y teología*, by various authors (San José, Costa Rica: Departamento Ecuménico de Investigaciones, 1986).

37. For this reason, in the great novel of Alejo Carpentier, *El reino de este mundo* (1949), Mackandal, the leader of the black rebellion, has to begin his insurrection strategy with full knowledge of the Haitian habitat, especially the potential use of poisonous plants.

38. For a theological treatment of the topic of the diaspora, see Carmelo Alvarez, *Una iglesia en diáspora: Apuntes para una eclesiología solidaria* (San José, Costa Rica: Departamento Ecuménico de Investigaciones, 1991).

39. Quoted by Paulo Suess, *Evangelizar desde los proyectos históricos de los otros: diez ensayos de misionología* (Quito: Ediciones Abya-Yala, 1995), p. 82. The reference is to a homily preached in 1633. The historian Carlos Esteban Deive points out that in the sixteenth century the majority of black slaves on Hispaniola died without receiving the sacrament of baptism. *La esclavitud del negro en Santo Domingo* (1492-1844), 2 vols.(Santo Domingo: Museo del Hombre Dominicano, 1980), p. 386. The Jesuit Alonso de Sandoval, at the beginning of the seventeenth century, vigorously censures the enormous neglect of the religious life of slaves. *Naturaleza, policia sagrada i profana, costumbres i ritos, disciplina i catecismo evangélico de todos etiopes* (Sevilla, 1627; 2da. Ed. Revisada, 1647). Reedited as *Un tratado sobre la esclavitud (introducción,* transcripción y traducción de Enriqueta Vila Vilar) (Madrid: Alianza Editorial, 1987).

40. Already in 1453, the Portuguese Gomes Eanes de Zurara appealed in his *Crónica de Guinea* to Noah's curse as the biblical text legitimizing the enslavement of Africans. Cf. Paulo Suess, "La esclavitud africana en las Américas," in the work by the same author, *Evangelizar desde los proyectos históricos de los otros,* pp. 27-52.

41. Regarding the importance of Carnival in the African Caribbean context, see Benítez-Rojo, *The Repeating Island*, pp. 22-29.

42. Alejo Carpentier, *Ecué-Yamba-Ó! Historia afrocubana* (Barcelona: Bruguera, 1980).
43. Juan Luis Segundo was aware of this for over two decades. In his book *Liberation of Theology* (Maryknoll, N.Y.: Orbis Books, 1976) he directed his glance in a very fruitful way to James Cone and the emerging "black theology," as an eminent example of what Segundo calls "the hermeneutic circle."
44. Alejo Carpentier, *El reino de este mundo* (Río Piedras, Puerto Rico: Editorial de la Universidad de Puerto Rico, 1994), p. 36.
45. Especially in *Los ríos profundos* (1958), *Todas las sangres* (1964), and his unfinished novel, *El zorro de arriba y el zorro de abajo* (1971).
46. I refer mainly to *El reino de este mundo* (1949), *Los pasos perdidos* (1953), and *Concierto barroco* (1974).
47. The central issue of Pentecostalism and its expansion in Latin America is beyond the scope of this essay. Richard Shaull has given a positive appraisal of this phenomenon in his essay "El quehacer teológico en el contexto de sobrevivencia en Abya-Yala" in *Por una sociedad donde quepan todos*, ed. José Duque, pp. 87-105. For his part, Harvey Cox argues that this growth cannot be reduced to a simple theological correlation of the expansion of market ideology. Cf. Harvey Cox, *Fire from Heaven: The Rise of Pentecostal Spirituality and the Reshaping of Religion in the Twenty-First Century* (Reading, Mass.: Addison-Wesley Publishing Co., 1995). Cox leaves open the question of whether, in certain sectors of Pentecostalism, one moves from the phase of the power of the Spirit to the more secular spirit of the Power.
48. In general, it can be affirmed that literature has been swifter than theology in perceiving its tangents with the religiosity of the peoples, than theology in becoming aware of the benefits it might obtain from a dialogue with Latin American narrative. An outstanding example is the Chilean-Costa Rican writer Tatiana Lobo, who in her novel *Calypso* (San José, Costa Rica: Editorial Norma, 1996) shows exceptional sensibility for the African American diaspora of the Central American Caribbean coast, its cultural affirmations, and its spirituality, and she does this with a fine sense of humor and irony, in addition to a seductive feminine eroticism. Lobo has written several other works (*Asalto al paraíso* [San José, Costa Rica: Editorial de la Universidad de Costa Rica, 1993] and *Entre Dios y el diablo* [San José, Costa Rica: Editorial de la Universidad de Costa Rica, 1993]) which also invite one to a creative dialogue with the new Latin American theological currents. About literature as a source for theological reflection, see the article by Vítor Westhelle and Hanna Betina Götz, "In Quest of a Myth: Latin American Literature and Theology," *Journal of Hispanic/Latino Theology*, vol. 3, no. 1, August 1995, pp. 5-22.
49. Cf. Pedro Trigo, "Arguedas: Mito, historia y religión" and Gustavo Gutierrez, "Entre las calandrias." Both are included in the same volume published by Centro de Estudios y Publicaciones, in Lima, in 1982. Gutierrez's essay is in large measure a response to the appeal which in his last novel Arguedas makes to him.
50. Alejo Carpentier, *Concierto barroco* (Río Piedras, Puerto Rico: Editorial de la Universidad de Puerto Rico. 1994), p. 72.
51. I have attempted to do a theological reading of the African-Antillean images and symbols in the literature of Alejo Carpentier in my essay, "*Mito, religiosidad e historia en Alejo Carpentier: Los ritmos sagrados de los pueblos afroamericanos,*" included in *Mito, exilio y demonios: Literatura y teología en América Latina* (San Juan: Publicaciones Puertorriqueñas, 1996), pp. 23-73.
52. José Lezama Lima, *La expresión americana*, pp. 53-56.
53. Cf. Lothar Coenen, Erich Beyreuther, Hans Bietenhard, *Diccionario teológico del Nuevo Testamento* (Salamanca: Ediciones Sígueme, 1983). vol. 3, pp. 438-445.
54. Edward W. Said, *Culture and Imperialism* (New York: Knopf, 1993), p. 108.
55. Gustavo Gutierrez, *En busca de los pobres de Jesucristo*, p. 276
56. Rubén Darío, *Cantos de vida y esperanza* (Madrid: Espasa-Calpe, 1976), pp. 68-69.

Glimpses of the
Missiology Consultation
San José, Costa Rica • April 21–25, 1997

from left: Eva Jensen, Vitalino Similox, Edwin Mora

from left: Raquel Rodriguez, Pablo Odén Marichal

from left: Miguel Gray, Silvia Regina de Lima Silva

from left: Rafael Malpica-Padilla, Bonnie L. Jensen

above from left: Ruth Orantes, Guillermo Kerber, Nancy Boye, Gloria Kinsler
below from left: Sarah Wiegner, Melissa Schellinger Gutiérrez

from left: Noemi Gorrin,
Daniel F. Romero,
Otilia Silva Leite

Stan Slade

from left:
Donald Reasoner,
Kermit J.De Graffenreidt

from left: Eva Jensen, Lillian Solt

from left: Carol Fouke, Maxine Sinclair, John Sinclair, Natan Pravia

from left: Noemi Gorrin, Edelberto Valdéz Fleites, Julia Ann Moffett

from left: Guillermo Encarnación, Aaron Gallegos

from left: Michael Rivas, Aldo Etchegoyen

from left: Adalia Gutiérrez, Sarah Wiegner, Vitalino Similox

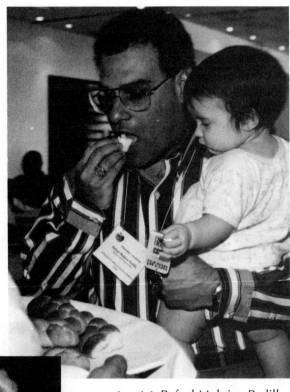

from left: Rafael Malpica-Padilla,
Melissa Schellinger Gutiérrez

Harvey Cox

from left: Mara Vidal, Guillermo Kerber

Timoteo Lima Quecana

Will L. Herzfeld

from left: McKinley Young and MOCRISCALEB, musical group from Venezuela

Mission in the Americas in the Twenty-first Century: A Northern Perspective

Harvey Cox

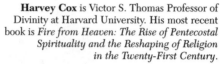

Harvey Cox is Victor S. Thomas Professor of Divinity at Harvard University. His most recent book is *Fire from Heaven: The Rise of Pentecostal Spirituality and the Reshaping of Religion in the Twenty-First Century.*

The mission of God's people is always and everywhere the same. It is also always and everywhere different. It is the same because the only mission we as God's people have is to continue, as best we can, the mission of Jesus Christ: the announcement and demonstration of the coming of God's promised reign of shalom. But it is also different because the historical circumstances within which it is carried on vary widely from age to age and place to place. Jesus Christ is the same yesterday, today, and forever. But Latin America in 1997 is not the same as Latin America in 1919. I will turn first to the mission, and then to the changed situation within which it must now be carried on. I will conclude with suggestions about how that might be done.

God's Shalom

The reign of God's shalom is always one in which the outsiders are invited in, the poor are satisfied, the sick are made whole, and the earth itself is renewed. The Old Testament prophets initiate this mission and lay the groundwork for its continuation. Throughout the Gospels, Jesus manifests the coming of God's shalom in both verbal and enacted parables, in deeds of mercy and healing, and in stern warnings to those who sinfully misuse power and privilege to deter the full realization of God's reign. After his death at the hands of those who represent the political, economic, and religio-cultural opposition to the coming of this reign, God raises Jesus from the dead as a vindication of God's mission and sends the Holy Spirit to empower men and women of faith to continue that mission.

The Panama Congress took place in 1916. That was the year—almost two decades after the calendar indicated it—that the nineteenth century was finally coming to its catastrophic end. It had been the great century of Western colonial and commercial expansion, the century in which the last of the European powers had achieved national unification, and the century in which the United States grew from a peripheral extension of Europe into what soon became history's mightiest superpower. It was also, not incidentally, the century of Western Christian missionary expansion into nearly every region of the world. The next decades would witness the end of one titanic and the coming of another; Fascism, Auschwitz, and Hiroshima; the achievement of political independence by the colonial world; and the rise and fall of Communism. It would also witness the emergence of powerful new economic, cultural, and religious forces—some of them toxic and some salutary—that shape the present era. Just as the Panama Congress occurred at the cusp of the nineteenth and twentieth centuries, this conference in San José, Costa Rica, occurs at the cusp of the twentieth and the twenty-first.

Today in Latin America, the mission of God's people continues to be the extension in history of God's purpose in sending Jesus Christ. The mission continues to meet with the same kind of opposition encountered by Jesus himself. That opposition still comes from those who misuse power—political, economic, religious, and cultural—to hinder the coming in its fullness of God's promised shalom. But also in Latin America today, God's people continue to be blessed with signs of God's sure and ultimate victory. Throughout the world, Christians look at Latin America with gratitude and wonder as a place where the gospel is being rediscovered and renewed with fresh power. Let us begin with the four elements of Jesus' own ministry:

The first is his unwavering commitment, announced at the outset of his ministry at Nazareth and consistently practiced until his crucifixion, to those who were excluded and deprived of their dignity by the ruling classes and institutions—both secular and religious—of his own day. Jesus demonstrated the love of a God who was on the side of the defeated and the heartbroken.

The second is Jesus' vision, further articulated by St. Paul, of the radically interdependent nature of the human community. We are the leaves and he is the vine. We are all one body in him. From his time in the womb of his mother to his removal from the cross (from the annunciation to the descent) Jesus showed that he needed other people to heal and teach just as they needed him. After Jesus' ascension, God empowered not a single successor but a people to carry on the mission.

The third element is the inclusiveness of that community, demonstrated by what some (borrowing a term from anthropology) have called his "open commensality." This inclusiveness expressed his blatant violation of the taboos that specified with whom one might share a meal, in order to make it clear that God welcomes everyone. This radical inclusiveness was powerfully demonstrated at Pentecost, when at the descent of the Holy Spirit, people who spoke a variety of languages were drawn together into one community without losing their distinctiveness.

The fourth element is Jesus' radical commitment to love and non-violence, his refusal, despite pressing temptations, to assume magical or coercive powers or resort to violence against other human beings in order to achieve his purposes. For Christians, the resurrection demonstrates that God's love is more powerful than that of the powers and principalities, and that, in principle, the victory is already won.

The question we face today is, How do we as the people of God continue *this mission* in the *new situation?* In particular, how do we continue it in Latin America where the two major forces shaping the continent are the "market revolution" (neoliberalism) and the rapid growth of Pentecostal Christianity? Let us now explore this new situation.

Living at a Turning Point

At the end of the second millennium after Christ's coming, God's people live at a turning point marked by dramatic changes in the nature of political, religious, and economic power. Some of these changes, such as the speed of travel and communication, offer unprecedented new opportunities for making the gospel known, just as the Pax Romana did in the first centuries of our era. But powerful interests still seek to deter the realization of God's shalom. Here are some specific changes that have altered the world since the Panama Congress:

1. In the *political realm* we see a growing popular distrust of the main vehicle through which political power has been brokered during the last three centuries—the national state. The reasons for this distrust are not hard to discern. Historically, national states emerged

by promising to give their people political independence and economic justice. But it is increasingly clear that they have accomplished neither. Modern weapons ignore national boundaries, as do epidemics, communications, and ecological catastrophes. With the ascent to global power of international corporations, national borders have become largely fictional. The International Monetary Fund (IMF) and the World Bank, not the national regimes, set the fundamental policies of many countries. Most governments have become "caretaker" regimes whose powers are severely delimited by what international market and financial experts will permit.

2. In the *economic realm*, nation states have failed even more dramatically. In their stead we have seen the emergence of a worldwide market structure controlled by private international corporations whose goal is not the national interest but profit. These corportions work so closely with international banking institutions that the elected governments of many countries have become little more than local custodians for these supranational powers. Paying the interest on their loans has become the largest item in the budgets of some poor countries. In 1996 the government of Uganda, to take only one example, spent $3 per person on health care and $17 per person repaying its foreign debt. In Uganda one in five children will not reach their fifth birthday, largely because of diseases that could be prevented through modest investment in primary health care. Many Latin American countries stagger under similar burdens. But even in countries like Germany and the United States, no government that ignores the decisions of those who determine what is a "favorable climate for investment" can hope to stay in power for long. The internationalization of the market, which began in Latin America with the European conquest, has now encircled the globe.

3. In the *cultural realm,* including the sphere of religion, new actors have come to the fore. They have gained influence because national states are in disrepute for failing to produce in the two key areas that warrant their existence, namely, political independence and economic justice. More and more people are removing their loyalty from nation states and investing it in other social and cultural formations. For large numbers of people, communities of race, religion, and ethnic origin—that often overlap—are increasing in importance as providers of a sense of memory, direction, and belonging. This trend helps explain the unexpected resurgence of

regionalism and the revival of spiritual movements all over the world, a century after Nietzsche prematurely declared that God was dead. Within Christianity, the most energetic and rapidly growing of these new religious movements is Pentecostalism. At the same time the global reach of mass media, almost entirely from North to South, is creating a universal culture of instant gratification, consumer values, and celebrity cults.

The people of Latin America are caught up in all these epochal changes. Although each change is significant, I will focus on two in particular. The first is what its neoliberal advocates call the "market revolution." It is important, especially at this conference, to emphasize that this "revolution" is inspired by the same kind of zeal that once propelled the Christian missionary movement. Its leaders are both tireless and genuinely dedicated to a vision. They are not motivated simply by avarice. Like earlier missionaries, they believe they have a saving message for all peoples: that the triumph of the market will end poverty and hunger once and for all. They are "market missionaries" who believe they have the answer.

The second change we need to consider is that, increasingly, the principal bearer of the Christian message, especially to the parts of the world where the market missionaries are at work, is the Pentecostal movement. In 1916 it was barely a decade old and had hardly begun its world-encircling trajectory. Now it includes more than 400 million people and is the fastest growing Christian movement on earth. If present trends continue, a pentecostalized expression of Christianity will dominate church life in the twenty-first century. This situation presents vast new opportunities and raises serious questions about the mission of God's people. It would be irresponsible to think about the Christian mission in the twenty-first century without pondering both the market missionaries and the Pentecostals. But even more importantly, we must probe the relationship between these two movements.

The Rise of Pentecostalism

Many have theorized about this relationship between Pentecostal-charismatic Christianity and the spread of market culture. One such theory, now almost universally discarded, was that of a nefarious conspiracy. Multinational corporations were scheming hand-in glove with Evangelical and Pentecostal missionaries to uproot hapless natives from their quaint indigenous rites and at the same time immunize them against the virus of liberation theology. The goal of this malicious strategy, it was alleged, was to destroy the two major barriers to market expansion—rooted traditionalism and religious egalitarianism—so that the target populations, like AIDS victims, would lack the white corpuscles needed to resist a market culture that requires mobility, undermines tradition, and promotes inequality as the price of prosperity.

Another theory held that the leaders of the Pentecostal-charismatic juggernaut were really entrepreneurs in disguise. They were in it only to peddle their tracts and shake down their naïve targets. It is true that televangelism is the quintessential capitalist achievement, in which the line between program and commercial, always thin at best throughout the industry, disappears completely. According to this theory, Pentecostalism is really business with a religious veneer.

But this theory is not persuasive either. Pentecostalism appears to be growing most rapidly precisely in the areas where North American power and money are least significant. China is the most dramatic example. Also, the vast majority of people drawn into Pentecostalism come not because of a televangelist but because a neighbor or relative invited them. Once having visited a congregation, they obviously find something they have been looking for. Furthermore, it is difficult to believe that nearly one half billion people have become Pentecostals because they are dupes or pushovers. There is something else happening here.

A third and far more sophisticated view of the link between the market revolution and the Christian religious upsurge holds that it was a kind of late-twentieth century reprise of the role earnest Methodists and Baptists played in the Industrial Revolution. This theory, advanced at one time by Peter Berger, among others, suggests that what the Pentecostals are doing is providing the same kind of work ethic of thrift, punctuality, and sobriety that supplied the reliable workforce for the satanic mills of the United Kingdom and the industrial expansion of the United States. In commenting on the zephyr-like spread of Pentecostalism in Latin America, for example, Berger writes, "What one may expect is that the new Protestant internationale will produce results similar to those of the preceding one—to wit, the emergence of a solid bourgeoisie, with virtues conducive to the development of capitalism."[1]

There are serious doubts about this theory, as well. In order to understand our mission in the next century, we will have to look deeper. It is now apparent that there are critical differences, not only between the current market revolution and the previous Industrial Revolution, but also between Pentecostalism—which is growing along with the market revolution—and the sectarian-Calvinist pietism that powered the missionary movements of the late nineteenth and early twentieth centuries. Furthermore, as one ponders the political situations in Singapore and mainland China, to say nothing of many countries in Latin America, the clearer it becomes that despite the hopeful rhetoric about free markets guarantee free elections, and the allegedly self-evident correlation of democracy with capitalism, the two seem all too easily separable in many places. Only the staunchest market missionary, for example, could claim that the North American Free Trade Agreement has improved the chances for democracy in Mexico. In fact, the most vigorous democratic forces in that country were inspired by opposition to NAFTA and to the corrupt PRI regime that sponsored it.

What distinguishes the present market revolution from the first Industrial Revolution is that the former is happening much faster and it is not being generated by a national elite but by multinational corporations. But why, one might ask, does a market economy require any kind of religious worldview? Why not just count on those sturdy old-fashioned virtues of greed and self-aggrandizement? Once again Peter Berger's work on "economic culture" moves us toward an answer. Capitalism, he points out, simply does not generate enough "mythopoetic" energy. It has never, one might say, inspired the songs it needs to celebrate its own qualities. And despite persistent efforts of advocates such as Michael Novak to crank up a theology of capitalism, nothing very convincing has ever come of the effort. Consequently, faced with contending mythic visions that hymn the glories of egalitarianism, socialism, or liberation, capitalism seems lackluster. It needs a little help from its friends. Clearly, advocates of the market culture hope that the ethos of the new Pentecostal-charismatic movement will supply just the cultural values the market missionaries need and without which they would falter.

Christians should be deeply suspicious of this logic. The market revolution, so far, has proven to be good news for a few but bad news for many more. Every culture in every age has had markets. Ours can hardly be an exception. When Jesus drove the money-changers from the temple, he was not leading an attack on the market as such but on the ways in which it created hardship for the poor and disfigured the religious values of his own faith. That is precisely the problem today. The Market (capital "M") has increasingly become the principal value-and-meaning-producing institution in the world. Its values—which might be suitable for the bazaar or even for large-scale businesses—are shaping neighborhoods, families, individuals, universities, and churches. Endless growth, clever merchandising techniques, and judging worth on the basis of cash value have become generalized. The traditional institutions—religion, family, local culture—that at one time guided, restrained, and limited the Market, have been enormously weakened, often by the impact of the Market itself.

Rather than blindly supporting market values or opposing any place for the market at all, Christians need to welcome markets when they truly enhance human life, but they must be prepared to warn against their subtle dangers. Most of all, we, as Christians, need to create and nurture human communities that are guided by gospel values, not by the values of accumulation and acquisition that are encouraged by the market culture. This need is what forces us to return to the biblical warrant for our mission. In this way, a new grasp of our past will help direct us into the future.

It is important to recall, as the Acts of the Apostles tells us, that immediately after Pentecost the first Christians organized themselves into a community that practiced an alternative economic system—one based on mutual sharing, not competition, accumulation, and gain. When Ananias and Sapphira were so severely punished, it was not for having heretical religious opinions but for violating the community's economic ethic.

The history of the Christian community in the first century is an important resource for us today. Like the early Christians, we, too, are living through not just a historical transition but a change in world-ages. As the year 2000 approaches, we are witnessing not just the end of a century but the end of an era—what the Roman Catholic theologian Romano Guardini once called *das Ende der Neuzeit*. Guardini meant that the icons of modernity—scientism, nationalism, technology, secularism—are no longer able to perform the quasi-religious function they assumed in the modern period. Consequently, what is now taking place is what Sigmund Freud, speaking about the individual, once called the "return of the repressed." In this situation, however, what has been "repressed" in our modern era is not sexuality but spirituality. Whereas Christian theology in the twentieth century has had to contend with atheism, skepticism, and the cultural "death of God," we are now living in a world of resurgent religious and spiritual vitality. The market culture itself has its spurious but highly seductive "spiritual" component, holding out promises of well-being, serenity, and worth.

Latin America today is living through a jarring period of massive uprooting and dislocation. Shaken loose from their traditional moorings, millions of people are caught between the past and the future and at the same time are deprived of the minimal resources they need for living in the present. It is all happening very quickly and it is this environment that often provides the richest soil for Pentecostal expansion. Part of the reason for Pentecostalism's appeal is that it permits people to hold on to something of the traditional symbolic world while at the same time coping with the new world. Today, many former practitioners of folk healing are Pentecostal preachers and healers, still practicing a healing art that stands both in continuity and in conflict with what they did before. In Korea the folk religion is shamanism, and significant elements of shamanic lore such as trance, exorcism, and mystical flight have been swept up into Pentecostal worship. The same bridging of past and present cultures is going on in sub-Saharan Africa, where dancing, drumming, and ancestor veneration—generally discouraged or forbidden by Protestants and Catholics—are welcomed into Pentecostal services. Pentecostalism is not a mere extension of fundamentalism. It is something quite different that, were its inner logic to play itself out, could completely subvert text-mediated religion. Pentecostals probably have more in common with St. Catherine of Siena than with John Calvin.

It is understandable that many observers can be misled about this bridging power of Pentecostalism, a capacity that contributes to its rapid growth. It is true, for example, that Pentecostal preachers often inveigh passionately *against* local indigenous religious practices. But at that very moment those same practices—dance, dream, healing, prophecy, ecstatic utterance—are erupting, often in a Christianized form, in Pentecostal worship itself. Try as these energetic preachers will to urge their people to turn their backs on the satanic forces around them—whether in Umbanda or shamanism or Vodun—the fact that they recognize the power of these forces demonstrates that these preachers, themselves, also affirm their reality. The people in the congregation may be grateful for the high wall erected by their strict moral codes between them and the dangerous and fallen world around them, but at the same time they see that spiritual world as a continuum of contending forces and clashing powers. Pentecostalism is the handrail over the abyss.

Because the tectonic plates underlying civilizations are shifting, chaos is one of the principal ways in which the poor experience the social landscape today. Pentecostal worship is a homeopathic cure. With it earsplitting noise and tumultuous prayer it challenges disorder on its own turf. It invites people to plunge into the chaos in order to overcome it by the power of the Holy Spirit. Unlike Protestants and Catholics, influenced by Enlightenment thinking, Pentecostals never claim that the spirits of the folk religion are illusory. Rather, they proclaim that God can defeat and vanquish them. This theology provides, ironically, both a bridge from the spiritual world of the old religion and a dam against its more sinister powers. But traffic on the bridge travels both ways, and the question of whether Pentecostalism is taming and assimilating the local shades or being assimilated by them is never fully decided. There are Pentecostals in the United States and Europe who have their doubts about whether some varieties of Korean Pentecostalism represent Christianized shamanism or shamanized Christianity. In any case, for millions of uprooted people around the world Pentecostalism clearly provides a symbolic safe place that enables them to survive the ravages of the new industrialization without completely abandoning their traditional symbolic world. This safety is one secret of its extraordinary growth.

As we think about the next century it is important to recognize that global Pentecostalism, contrary to what many of its critics claim, is not just a new edition of Fundamentalism. In fact, the power of Pentecostalism can be understood most clearly at the point at which it *differs* from classical Fundamentalism. Indeed, when Pentecostalism first emerged in its present form during the famous Azusa street revival that began in Los Angeles in 1906—at first among black custodians and domestic servants, soon attracting lower-class whites as well—the Fundamentalists were among its most vociferous critics. One of these antagonists, using a phrase Pentecostals have not forgotten over the century, called them the "last vomit of Satan." Spurned and ridiculed by the downtown churches as "Holy Rollers," they were attacked even more vehemently by Fundamentalist who were afraid that the Pentecostal belief in a direct, unmediated experience of God would undercut the authority of doctrine.

This disagreement should not come as a surprise to students of the history of religion. Pentecostals are, after all, populist mystics, and text-oriented religions throughout the millennia have had a problem with mystics. Fundamentalists and conservative Christians also stridently disagreed with the Pentecostals' claim that miracles still occur in the present age. Not long after Pentecostals appeared on the scene, one stern Princeton Presbyterian naysayer declared that because they believed in contemporary miracles they were just as bad as Catholics. In this judgment, incidentally, he unintentionally foreshadowed some more recent sociological analyses which suggest that, in fact, Pentecostalism, especially in Latin America, might better be understood as a mutation not of evangelical Protestantism but of popular folk Catholicism. Pouring into the huge, intimidating cities of the continent from the impoverished countryside, the new arrivals reconstitute fragments of their previous lives, including its popular Catholicism, as best they can. In the midst of the jarring urban confusion they can still find miracles and healing in one of the Pentecostal congregations, and a welcoming company of new brothers and sisters to replace the *comprades* left behind in the village. The pastor becomes the surrogate *patron*, and they can even reclaim some of the exhilaration of the fiesta in the dancing and singing of the nightly prayer meetings. The Mexican religious historian Jean-Pierre Bastian may exaggerate, but he makes a valuable point when he calls the Pentecostals "Catholics without priests."

A Return of Spirituality

We are still left with a question. Why is it Pentecostalism and not some other expression of Christianity that is growing so rapidly in precisely the same areas where the market revolution is sweeping ahead? Our answer could help to clarify our thinking about Christian mission in the next century.

Some observers suggest that because of the authoritarian structure of their polity, Pentecostals feel comfortable about accepting the same authoritarian style as that in society at large. Market missionaries sometime insist that capitalism at this stage of its development must not be burdened with "an excess of democracy," so they welcome religiously imbued deference to "those in charge." They also believe that since Pentecostalism cultivates a direct and individual relationship with God, it promotes the kind individualism that the market requires. Its highly emotional worship also encourages desire for a kind of immediate gratification—a spiritual version of a state of mind that is knowingly played on by the alluring advertisements of the local supermarket. They believe, in short, that Pentecostalism is almost tailor-made for the consumer culture, just as ascetic Protestantism was suited to an earlier stage of capital accumulation. The market missionaries, in brief, encourage Pentecostalism not because they yearn for the gifts of the Spirit but because they think Pentacostalism will move goods. It will help bring about the spread of market culture.

There may, indeed, be something in that view, but I believe the relationship between the new Pentecostal expansion and the market revolution is far more complex. The standardization and homogenization of mass capitalist culture deprives people of genuine experience. How is this deprivation connected to the massive return of the experiential Christianity offered by Pentecostal worship? That same mass culture also thins out community and encourages individualism. Though Pentecostalism is sometimes accused of fomenting individualism, its converts report time and time again that they have discovered a new and powerful sense of belonging. Most frequently they describe the other people in their congregation as brothers and sisters. Through its ceaseless advertising onslaught, market culture relies heavily on pandering to the images of the life it says we should all aspire to. But part of Pentecostalism's power is its attack on the perverse values of "this fallen age." Although they have frequently made compromises with this conviction, the early Pentecostals were determined not to be seduced by the "wiles of this world." Recently, some Pentecostal leaders have tried to revive this rejection of "worldliness" as a powerful critique of consumer culture. Clearly, there are elements in the Pentecostal worldview that do not comport well with market capitalism.

But that is not the whole story. Pentecostals often act in just the way that the market missionaries hope they will. Pentecostals has its cadres of "name it and claim it" preachers who tell their people that if they are not rich, it is their own fault for not trusting God enough. Just as in an earlier wave of Protestantism, when Pentecostals become middle class, they often forget that their original mission was to the poor. Although their movement began on the wrong side of the tracks among poor whites and even poorer blacks, many

Pentecostals would prefer to forget that history and climb up the echelons of power and privilege, on the backs of others if necessary.

Still, on balance, the growth of Pentecostalism offers more positive than negative possibilities for the future of the Christian world mission. Most important, it has provided us with a powerful new metaphor. During the last decades of the twentieth century, the "Exodus paradigm" provided the main illumination for mission. But today the Exodus story is only of limited use. Its strength is that it is about truth confronting power: Moses against Pharaoh. Its weakness is that it tells a story about a new start *elsewhere*, and today there is no elsewhere. This lack is why Christians are rediscovering what might be called the "Pentecost paradigm." This paradigm does not mean simply that various forms of Pentecostalism are becoming the numerically predominant form of our faith today, or even that the main influence of the Pentecostal tide may be within other—evangelical, ecumenical and Catholic—Christian movements, although both of these are true. The Pentecost paradigm means that at the outset of Christian history the Holy Spirit empowered a community that drew peoples of various cultures into itself, without depriving them of their cultural identities, and at the same time refused to be swept into the economic culture of its own day. The paradigm is the power to forge an inclusive new community, not elsewhere but here, and at the same time to stand against the leveling and homogenizing power of the reigning economic culture. It is a power Christians believe comes from God alone. It is the power that came to the Christian community at Pentecost and it is the key biblical insight for our time, especially in Latin America. The question remains: Will Pentecostals—and other Christians, as well—allow ourselves merely to be swept along by the consumer-market culture, together with its destructive values? Or will we reclaim the power of this Pentecost paradigm?

End Note

1. As quoted in the introduction to David Martin, *Tongues of Fire: The Explosion of Protestantism in Latin America* (Blackwell Publishers, 1990).

The Incarnation of Faith in African American Culture: The Struggle for Minority Rights in the North

Jeremiah Wright

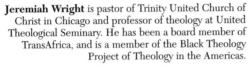

Jeremiah Wright is pastor of Trinity United Church of Christ in Chicago and professor of theology at United Theological Seminary. He has been a board member of TransAfrica, and is a member of the Black Theology Project of Theology in the Americas.

Forty-five years ago Ralph Ellison, in his classic novel, *The Invisible Man,* put his finger on a reality with which I have been wrestling since at least 1955. Let me explain. I grew up in a town with two YMCAs. There was one YMCA for white people and one YMCA for African Americans. This was quite confusing to me, because the "C" in YMCA stands for "Christian." There were two Christian organizations.

The black Christian YMCA did not have a swimming pool. The white one did. Blacks, however, could not swim in the white one except on certain days of the week. I made the mistake of walking into the white "Y" one day and learning quite abruptly that my skin was the wrong color. I asked my parents about it and they tried to explain to me (I was ten years old) what white racism meant and how white Christians "just didn't get it."

The Jesus my parents knew, however, (the Incarnation of Faith), was not a Jesus that white Christians knew. That caused me, at least forty-two years ago, to reflect on the schizophrenic existence of African Americans living in a racist country and trying to profess Christ as Lord.

Ellison's primary theme was that African Americans were invisible in American culture. Invisible to those who wrote history. Invisible to those who made political decisions. Invisible to those who did theology, and invisible to those of the dominant culture who practiced this faith we call Christianity. Entire histories have been written as though we did not exist. We were invisible. We did not count.

Dr. John Kinney, dean of the School of Theology at Virginia Union University, says, "We have moved from 1787, when we didn't count in the Constitution of the United States. We were invisible; we were three-fifths of a man. We have moved from there to the place in 1997 where we don't matter. Our culture doesn't matter. Our history doesn't matter. Our story doesn't matter. Our perspective doesn't matter. Our very existence doesn't matter. We are still invisible."

You will hear this reality masked behind phrases and slogans such as "multiculturalism," or "a color-blind society," or in Michael Jackson's "It Makes No Difference if You're Black or White." It doesn't matter! It doesn't matter what color you are. Some people even say, "When I look at you I don't see color."

Either they are lying or they are in serious denial. We are still invisible. We have moved from the place where we didn't count to the place where we don't matter. What our people went through in the terrible holocaust of the West African slave trade—where not 6 million, but 100 million were lost—doesn't matter.

I heard the head of the African studies department at the University of South Florida say during Black History Month, "Even the language of the dominant culture tries to hide the truth rather than speak the truth concerning the West's attitudes toward people of African descent." She quoted from a 1996 text in American history used by the university, which says, "The increased demand for sugar and cotton . . . necessitated the Atlantic Slave Trade." Consider the obfuscation of truth—the hiding of the hideous inhumanity of English and European peoples against Africans in that sentence, as it dances around the truth.

"The increased demand for sugar and cotton . . ." Who was demanding sugar and cotton? The Africans working in the cotton fields? The Africans slaving on the sugar plantations? Who demanded the increase? The textbook authors can't bring themselves to tell the truth: that the demand arose because somebody (unnamed!) wanted more sugar and more cotton. Could this be the free market economy? The impersonal and unbiased gospel of greed? It was necessary because somebody wanted more sugar and more cotton. It was necessary. This makes it right. Necessitated, indeed!

Even the language of the dominant culture tries to hide the truth rather than speak out concerning the West's attitudes toward Africans and people of African descent. What our people went through in the holocaust of the African slave trade does not matter. What our women suffered as they were raped does not matter.

Do you know the story of a town in Senegal called San Louis? Almost a decade ago, my wife and I were in Senegal. I could not understand why the Senegalese looked at me strangely every time I spoke to them. They spoke to my wife, but not to me. I asked our Muslim guide the reason, and he smiled and answered, "Would you like to see San Louis? That will explain the matter much more graphically than any explanation I could give."

We made the trip to San Louis and found a town full of persons of my complexion. I am a light-skinned African American. My wife is a dark-brown skinned African American. What we discovered on that trip—and what our guide further explained to us—was that during the height of the slave trade, African women would try to get pregnant by white (European) slave traders because they knew that if they were pregnant they would not be put on ships and sent away from their homes forever.

The offspring of these unions, however, were part African and part Spanish, or French, Dutch, English, or German—depending on which slave trader or slave ship captain had impregnated their mothers. The children were not accepted by the Africans and they were not accepted by the Europeans. They became a class or caste of their own and established a culture all their own. Native Africans, as a result, were not used to speaking to light-skinned Africans (mixed-breed people of a lineage harking back to the days of slavery); and they were not used to people of light-skinned complexion speaking to them. That is why they looked at me so strangely when I spoke.

The conscious decision made by African women to sleep with the enemy rather than suffer in slavery, does not matter.

What Harriet Tubman, an African Methodist Episcopal Zion minister, lived through, and the decisions she made concerning violence versus passive resistance—carrying a .44 to enforce solidarity in the quest for liberation—does not matter.

What Jarena Lee, another African Methodist Episcopal minister, lived through as she fought both the racism in America and the sexism of her own people, does not matter.

What David Walker lived through and wrote about; what Bishop Henry McNeal Turner lived through, preached, and taught; what Gabriel Prosser, Denmark Vesey, and Nat Turner preached; what Gullah Jack and Macandal had in common both theologically and spiritually—how Africans changed the history of the entire Western Hemisphere, defeating the armies of France by using spiritual practices—none of that matters, for it is not taught in the majority of our seminaries, divinity schools, or churches.

The similarities in music, dance, and theology between Obeah (in Jamaica), Cumina (in Belize and Costa Rica), Candomblé (in Bahia), Vodun (in Haiti), Santéria (in Cuba), Shango (in Trinidad), and the Azuza Street Revival in Los Angeles are not talked about, explored, explained, or even examined in most Western Christian circles. After all, as Ellison pointed out, we are invisible. Either we don't count or we don't matter. This is true even in my field of the history of religions (I spent six years at the University of Chicago studying under Dr. Mircea Eliade and Dr. Charles Long), because Africans in the New World were "invisible"—a kind of backdrop against which were painted the great Western religions, themes, and movements.

The Protestant Reformation began during the rape of African countries. The Oxford Movement and Congregationalism flourished as the West African slave trade flourished. The Great Awakening and the Second Great Awakening were carried out by slave-holding preachers of the gospel. Africans were fixtures—part of the flora and fauna of the Great Discovery and settling of the New World, or so it seems when you read the narratives of American church history. And because Africans were "invisible," even in my field, we almost missed one of the greatest discoveries right under our noses—and we couldn't see it because of the opacity of the Africans among us.

On the one hand, there was this vast area of African history and Africans in the history of the Americas before Columbus that was untouched in North American history classes, and, in far too many instances, is still not taught in Central America, South America, or the Caribbean.

I had to read a book on Panamanian history (en Español!) to find out about my own people, to find out that Africans had been to this continent before slavery, before Columbus, and before the Spanish and Italian "discovery" of the West. In 1508, according to one Panamanian textbook, when Balboa "discovered" the Native Americans in Panama (I believe they were the Arawak), he noticed that their spears were tipped with gold, and having a great thirst for gold, he asked casually what it was called and where it came from. The Native Americans said it was "Gana," brought here and traded by men from Gana (Ghana). The Ghanaians had been sailing to and trading with countries in Central America centuries before the Europeans, but my North American (United States) textbooks did not teach me that.

On the one hand, there was this vast area of pre-Columbian history of Africans and of Africans in the Americas. The step pyramids and the giant African heads at Dos Zapotes and Las Treintas point to that history. It is a history our textbooks do not mention, because it would call for a radical reinterpretation of people we had labeled ignorant, subhuman, culturally deprived, backward, and in need of our Western civilization. It is a history that was just not taught in North America, where the stereotypes against blacks still reign supreme (affecting the ideology, the theology, and the sociology of missiology, which we will discuss in a moment). On the other hand, there were startling signs of Africans who were Christians and who were practicing Christianity in a different way from the way Westerners had authorized. We almost let that truth get completely past us!

Here is how it happened, and here is how attempts have been made to reverse this tragic trend. Because Africans were invisible—because they didn't count and because they didn't matter—there was the automatic (or arrogant) assumption that Africans came here with a *tabula rasa*. Their minds, it was assumed, were empty chalkboards, and nothing significant appeared on those chalkboards until Spanish, Portuguese, English, Dutch, or French owners, traders, teachers, missionaries, or preachers began to write on them.

That was the assumption. By extension, it was also assumed that Africans became Christian either through the catechisms of the Anglican and Roman Catholic communions, the Society for the Propagation of the Gospel in Foreign Parts beginning in 1702, or the evangelistic work of a few committed white brothers and sisters in the Caribbean or South America.

It is crucial to keep in mind the nature of the Triangular Trade in order to understand the cultures, the languages and their creolization, the music, the faith, and the religious practices of Africans in the three Americas. The cross-fertilization and the hybridization, to use Dr. Cornel West's term, cannot be lightly dismissed.

But the assumption on the part of white historians, white church persons, and blacks trained in those traditions (to which we will return in a moment), was that Africans became Christians because of slavery. Not a thought was given to the possibility that there might have been some African Christians before slavery or before their exposure to the racist dogma that passed itself off as Christianity.

Nor was any thought given to the obvious fact that the way in which Africans understood Christianity (their theology and their hermeneutic), and the way in which Africans practiced

Christianity—in terms of their worship services as well as their struggle against slavery—meant that African Christianity and European or English Christianity were two different things altogether.

Blaine Ramsey, a preacher to African slaves, observed in the early 1780s that the religion of the slave and the religion of the slave holder were, by definition, two different religions: the God of the slave and the God of the slave holder, and the faith of the slave and the faith of the slave holder were two different Gods and two different faiths. When the Word became flesh for Africans held in slavery, it meant something vastly different from what it meant to the ones who were holding them.

Although Ramsey pointed out the obvious, what most church historians, most theologians, and most sociologists of religions kept missing was just that—the obvious. If Christianizing slaves made them better slaves, and if evangelizing Africans with slave catechisms made them more docile and much less likely to revolt, and if a converted slave was a contented slave—singing those beautiful spirituals around the veranda while massa and missy drank mint julep—why were there hundreds of slave revolts led by African Christians? Why did Africans keep slipping away to freedom, stealing away to freedom, and using their religious songs as signals in the running of the Underground Railroad? Why was Gabriel Prosser a Baptist preacher? Gullah Jack a conjure man? Why were Dessalines and Macandal practitioners of Vodun? Why was David Walker a steward in the African Methodist Episcopal Church? Why was Denmark Vesey an elder in the AME church, and why were Nat Turner, a Baptist minister, and Harriet Tubman, a minister of the AME Zion church, both violent practitioners of the Christian faith?

Why did Africans keep sneaking out to the woods to their brush arbors or hush arbors to hold secret worship services? What were they doing during those worship services that was so different from those of their services that were observed by whites? What didn't they want whites to see?

What was going on? Of course because they were invisible, because they did not count, and because they did not matter, almost nobody thought to ask until it was almost too late.

It was not until the 1960s, one hundred years after the end of North American slavery, that such questions were raised, and by then almost all of the Africans who had lived in slavery or who had been born in slavery were dead , so they could not be asked the crucial questions. Fortunately, however, there was (and still is) a corpus of literature collected by the Works Project Administration that is invaluable for gleaning the kinds of responses that we had overlooked for thirty years (and many of us, for sixty years).

During the depression years in the United States the government sent out hundreds of people to record the stories of Native Americans (Seminole, Choctaw, Apache, Sioux, Comanche, Arapaho, Navajo, Blackfoot, and Pueblo) and hundreds of others to record the stories of Africans who had lived in slavery. For the most part, those slave narratives just sat, ignored by blacks and whites alike. Most whites ignored them because Africans did not count. Most blacks ignored them because they had been taught to look down their noses at anything African, anything from slavery, anything ignorant, pagan, or heathenish—and those pages from African American history were considered just that.

What the slave narratives have taught us is that Africans were practicing Christianity in their own way. The Word, indeed, had become flesh for them and given them a faith with the dual face of liberation and celebration. What the slave masters had taught, what the slave preachers had preached, and what the slave culture had practiced, Africans viewed as pure nonsense—an abomination before God and hypocrisy at its zenith. One of their spirituals used to say it this way:

> I got shoes, you got shoes,
> All God's children got shoes.
> When I get to heb'n gonna put on my shoes,
> Gonna walk all over God's heb'n.
> Everybody talkin' 'bout heb'n ain't going there. Heb'n.

Whites talking about heaven while practicing slavery were not going there. Whites holding the Bible in one hand and a slave in the other were not going to heaven. Africans who shared an oral-aural culture had heard the gospel: "Inasmuch as ye have done it unto the least of these my little ones, ye have done it unto me." They had heard the gospel and they had met the risen Lord themselves. They had experienced the Holy Ghost. They had been freed by the power of God, and, once freed on the inside, no chains could hold them on the outside. The Word becoming flesh for them (in chains) meant something far different from what it meant to those holding the chains.

Their worship services, secret and clandestine, ushered in a perspective of proleptic eschatology. They were given a foretaste of how things were going to be by and by (after a while). Their celebration energized them to seek liberation, and so they did. Some went North. Some went into the swamps with the Seminole. Some went into the West with the Apache, and some stayed right where they were and set others free. This duality of celebration and liberation can be traced all the way from the slave narratives up through the civil rights movement and the Million Man March of 1995.

But time will not permit that treatment in this essay. Here I want to call your attention to missiology and the negative effect it has had upon Africans living in the North American diaspora. It is almost common knowledge now that until the past twenty-five to thirty years missionaries assumed, for the most part, that they were civilized and that the objects of their mission work were uncivilized. It was also taken for granted that Western European or English culture was superior to African culture, and that "white" culture was equated with Christianity. Giving Africans white culture, therefore, was synonymous with giving them Christianity.

While most in this gathering are painfully familiar with this reality in Latin America, many of us miss the extent to which it has shaped reality for Africans living in North America. Let me talk to you about the American Missionary Association, the body that did the lion's share of mission work among blacks and Indians in the United States of America. Before 1865, the American Missionary Association and the Congregational Church were very active abolitionists. They were active in the abolition movement, and were fiercely committed to abolishing slavery and getting Africans out of slavery. They actively participated in the Underground Railroad. Several ministers and members of the Congregational Church became conductors (Harriet Tubman was one) and maintained stations on the Underground Railroad. After 1866, when the war had ended, and through 1870, the American Missionary Association established more than five hundred schools and churches in the South.

A massive problem arose when the "freedmen" were turned loose with absolutely no skills to sustain them. In most of the states it had been against the law to teach Africans how to read. It had been against the law to educate Africans. Now there were millions of un-educated and untrained persons.

The United Church of Christ, through its predecessor denomina-tion, the Congregational Church, and specifically through the American Missionary Association, sent hundreds of missionaries into the South to address a refugee problem and a serious problem of education. The American Missionary Association was organized under the dictum, "Evangelicalism Through Education and Acculturation": education (meaning Eurocentric blindness, reinforc-ing the essence of invisible Africans) and acculturation (meaning that you must become like us in order to be saved; in order to have any worth or in order to be of any value).

The more that blacks became like whites, the more accepted we were, and so the double consciousness of W. E. B. DuBois became a painful reality, denying who we were in order to be accepted by those who looked upon us as unacceptable. We didn't count. We didn't matter. We were invisible.

And so blacks taught by missionaries began to disdain and deni-grate their own history, their own story, their own music, their own culture. This caused a major rift in the African American communi-ty—a rift that exists to this day.

Common-meter singing, a form of black hymnody that became popular in the 1800s, was disdained by Africans who were striving now—thanks to the missionaries—to be accepted by whites. All forms of black singing were outlawed in "respectable" churches. Not even spirituals as sung by Africans were allowed. Only "arranged" spirituals and concertized, anthemic spirituals were acceptable. The Fisk Jubilee Singers popularized this form of singing—a form con-sidered acceptable by whites. It is ironic that the home of the singers, Fisk University, is one of the AMA colleges. It is these spirituals and anthems that became the fare that made a church "respectable."

No gospel music was sung on any black campus in the United States of America until 1968. Created in the 1920s, gospel music is a fusion of blues, jazz, and spirituals. Yet it was not considered "acceptable" because it made people want to move, tap their feet, sway, and express their feelings bodily. The missionaries had taught us that such expression of emotion was unacceptable. They had taught us that black music was not sacred music. They had taught us that singing such music, handclapping, and bodily expression were not the way to worship God "aright."

Bishop Daniel Payne, educated at a Lutheran seminary, said to one of his overseers in the African Methodist Episcopal Church in South Carolina, "We have got to stomp out this 'fist and heel' music." He meant the kind of music in which Africans kept the beat going by pounding their fists in their hands and stomping with their feet. That was not European. That was not what the missionaries accepted, and that was not "respectable" enough to make us accepted by the dominant culture. Bishop Payne's presiding elder, an African from the Sea Coast Islands, said, "Bishop, without the beat the spirit don't come." To paraphrase the biblical phrase, "The Word becomes rhythm and dwells among us."

Yet, the ring shout, the Pentecostal spiritualism, the joy of celebration, and the struggle for liberation persist. Most of you don't know what the ring shout is. The ring shout is a form of worship that Africans used in this country as early as the 1700s.

Thomas Wentworth Higginson writes about this cultural artifact in his book *Army Life in a Black Regiment*. Higginson was a white officer in command of a black regiment during the War for Independence in 1776. He writes about his experience as the commander of a group of Africans who were fighting for the colonies in that war. In their free time the Africans worshiped, they practiced their oral tradition, they sang, and they did the ring shout. The ring shout can still be found today among descendants of the Gullah tradition in the islands off the coast of South Carolina and Georgia.

Several years ago, when we arrived in Cote d'Ivoire for the first African-African American Summit, the Ivorians welcomed us by doing one of their traditional dances. One of the AME ministers from Charleston, South Carolina, exclaimed, "It's the ring shout!" The summit participants answered, "Of course it is! Where do you think that dance came from? It came from right here in West Africa."

Though there had been efforts by educated (that is, missionary-educated) blacks—really meaning assimilated or acculturated blacks—to stamp out the Africanisms in our faith tradition, the ring shout and the "pentecostal" spiritualism within the African church community in North America persist. They persist because educated, uneducated, or miseducated Africans (to use Carter G. Woodson's term)[1] who have experienced the risen Christ, the Incarnate Word, and the One who accepts them as they are—those who have been touched by the Spirit (or, to quote Alejo Carpentier once again [see Rivéra-Pagan essay]), "The Bible once again became rhythm and dwelt among us"—those who have been touched by that Spirit hear a different drummer when they hear the words, "If the Son shall set you free, you shall be free, indeed."

Because the sons and daughters of African descent hear "a different drummer," they sing along with the Africans who stole away to be free:

> And before I'd be a slave—
> a slave to demeaning theologies,
> a slave to racist sociology,
> a slave to sexism or capitalism . . .
>
> And before I'd be a slave,
> I'll be buried in my grave
> and go home to my Lord and be free!"

End Note

1. Carter G. Woodson's classic work, *The Miseducation of the Negro* (Trenton, N. J. : Africa World Press, 1990), explains that what we have been calling education in North America is actually miseducation. Africans have been miseducated away from their culture, away from their center, and away from themselves. They have been taught that anything European is right and that anything African is wrong. They have been taught all about Europe and nothing about Africa.

God's Mission, Our Mission: Latin America at the Dawn of the Third Millennium

F. Ross Kinsler

F. Ross Kinsler, a missionary of the Presbyterian Church (USA), is professor of theology and missiology at the Latin American Biblical Seminary, San José, Costa Rica.

At every point in history and now with some urgency at the dawn of a new millennium, we do well to clarify God's mission and, thus, our mission in this world. The social and human sciences provide important perspectives and instruments for such reflection, but ultimately we must use our own biblical, theological, and missiological sciences to clarify our mission and evaluate and question what we are doing and how we are living in the face of it.

I do not pretend to define for others what their mission should be. Rather, I have taken a personal approach based on experiences and reflections in Central America and North America during the last thirty-three years. I hope that these words will stimulate others to share their experiences and reflections on the basis of their biblical, theological, and missiological vision.

In this presentation I shall draw on the three points of the hermeneutical circle. First, I shall present a vision of the world, "a world where there is room for all," as the Zapatistas of Chiapas say. Another version of this slogan is, "What we want is a world where there is room for many worlds." Second, I shall consider a vision of the biblical faith in the words of Jesus: "Seek first God's reign and God's justice" (Matthew 6: 33). I shall use the Jubilee as a key to the ancient and present interpretation of this reign. And third, as a complement and fulfillment of these two fundamental points, I will propose a vision of our mission as "the option for and from the excluded ones" in the face of current ideologies, structures, and mechanisms of domination and marginalization.

A Vision of the World: "A World Where There Is Room for All"

Much has been written about "the new world order" inaugurated by the collapse of the socialist regimes, the end of the cold war, and the so-called triumph of capitalism, not to mention "the end of history." In Latin America, we have seen profound and alarming analyses of the socioeconomic impact of the globalized market. It is becoming more and more evident at every level and in all sectors of our life. The United Nations Program on Human Development has published ample statistics proving that the current world economic model is accelerating the concentration of wealth—material, human, and technological resources—and deepening and broadening the levels of poverty on all continents.

For some, these changes have revealed the inadequacy or irrelevance of Latin America's liberation theology. Others think that this vision of the world developed during the 1970s and 1980s is more relevant than ever—though insufficient. The accelerating concentration of wealth and power and the increasing marginalization of the poor and powerless are overwhelming historical realities. The important contribution of liberation theology during the last thirty years has been its analysis of capitalism and the proclamation of the socioeconomic and theological-pastoral liberation from the capitalist system, which it offers as the option for the poor. Today this analysis of marginalization and exclusion is being widened and deepened by including the categories of gender, race, culture, nationality, social location, and functional and mental condition. The option for the marginalized and excluded is still important, and the economic category is still fundamental. Thus many—those who are advocates of liberation theology as well as others— are using the slogan of the Zapatistas, proposing a vision "for a world where there is room for all."

As biblical-theological grounding for this vision, I would like to use Walter Wink's research on principalities and powers in his trilogy, *Naming the Powers, Unmasking the Powers,* and *Engaging the Powers.* On the basis of exhaustive studies of New Testament language, Wink concludes that in many passages the word *world* (cosmos) should be translated or interpreted as "the domination system," which he defines as "the human sociological realm that exists in estrangement from God."[1] Thus, Jesus tells his brothers to go to the

Feast of Tabernacles without him, because "the domination system cannot hate you, but it hates me because I testify against it that its works are evil" (John 7:7). Similarly, Jesus says to the scribes and the Pharisees, "You are from below, I am from above; you are of this domination system; I am not of this domination system" (John 8:23). In 1 John 4:5, the writer explains that the enemies of God "are from the domination system, and the domination system listens to them." At the end of his ministry, when Jesus is on trial for his life, he responds to the high priest, the supreme representative of the system of religious, social, economic, and political domination, "I have spoken openly to the domination system: I have always taught in synagogues and in the Temple" (John 18:20). Later he stands before the Roman governor, Pilate, and testifies, "My kingdom is not from this domination system" (John 18:36). Thus, Jesus' disciples are, likewise, to reject the domination system, for "those who hate their life in this domination system will keep it for eternal life" (John 12:25, cf. Mark 8:36). "The domination system and its desire are passing away, but those who do the will of God live forever" (1 John 2:17)

The world (cosmos) created by God is, of course, very good (Genesis 1:31), but the domination system (cosmos) is evil. "We know that we are God's children and that the whole domination system lies under the power of the evil one" (1 John 5:19). Jesus has overcome this domination system through his life and his crucifixion. Before the final trial he tells his disciples, "In the domination system you face persecution. But take courage; I have conquered the domination system!" (John 16:33). Likewise, Paul testifies, "May I never boast of anything except the cross of our Lord Jesus Christ, by which the domination system has been crucified to me, and I to the domination system" (Galatians 6:14). And he presents this same call to the believers of Corinth in these terms. "God chose what is foolish in the domination system to shame the wise" (1 Corinthians 1:27). Likewise, James writes, "Has not God chosen the poor in the domination system to be rich in faith and to be heirs of the kingdom that he has promised to those who love him?" (James 2:5).

Wink is convinced that the United States has succumbed to the domination system, institutionally and individually. This submission is expressed externally through obsessive militarism and economic imperialism and internally through sexism and racism. He even affirms that this domination system is the primary religion in the United States, whatever our diverse secondary religious beliefs and church affiliations may be. So, the struggle for liberation in the United States and the world is centered in ourselves, individually and collectively. And it must challenge our understanding of biblical faith, our theology, our churches, and our practice of mission. The struggle for liberation is the struggle for a world in which there is room for all.

Four years ago the Caribbean Baptist Theological Center (now CTC) was inaugurated in Limon, the principal Atlantic port of Costa Rica. It began with very limited economic resources but with the support of the local Baptist church. At first it had to struggle to gain the cooperation of the thirteen Baptist churches in the region, and now includes—in addition to Baptists—Methodists, Episcopalians, Pentecostals, and students from other denominations. The name "Baptist " has been dropped. All of Limon's churches are very conservative, pietistic, and "spiritual," and keep themselves apart from the social, economic, political, and daily life of their own people. Limon has been identified with the black population of Costa Rica; it is the most abandoned region of the country, although it is also the region that produces the greatest wealth because of its seaport and as a producer of bananas and coffee.

Several months ago, the CTC offered a course in social analysis and the theological task. Each student chose an area for research—women, ecology, economics, and so forth—in the context of Limon. Those who studied the economic reality of the city investigated the situation of the stevedores. The government wanted to privatize and automate the port, lay off many stevedores, and thus lower costs in order to increase competitiveness and profits for the export-import companies, applying the ideology of free trade and the dictates of the International Monetary Fund (IMF) and the World Bank. When the students discovered the effects of these changes on the lives of the stevedores' families, they organized a meeting with them and some pastors and church leaders. Thus began conversations that produced a new spirit of solidarity with those affected. Ultimately, members of fifty-six organizations gathered to protest, not only on behalf of the stevedores but a whole range of other demands related to health, education, housing, roads, sewers, employment, and so forth, with the slogan, "Limon en Lucha" (Limon's Struggle). This movement went far beyond the Caribbean Theological Center. It led to public demonstrations and police repression, and was finally resolved through accords signed in the office of the President of

Costa Rica. The whole affair did much to persuade theological students, the pastors and leaders, the churches, and especially the stevedores and their families that biblical faith has much to do with this world and its systems of domination and with the struggle for a world that has room for all.

A Vision of Biblical Faith: The Reign of God and God's Justice

The struggle against exclusion poses a major challenge to our faith and our churches. The so-called historic churches that have traditionally occupied a privileged position in the North ("mainline" churches) and that presume to have a certain superiority in the South as well, have been losing strength and position (retreating to the "sideline").Their efforts in support of economic, racial, and social justice appear to be more and more limited as perceived by the outside world and the churches themselves. In their place other movements and church models are emerging that seem more suited to, and more successful in, today's culture. They include new charismatic expressions, megachurches, theatrical religious music, television evangelists, an emphasis on the theology of prosperity, and high-powered campaigns for funds and members.

In order to clarify our vision of God's mission—our mission—we need to ask what Jesus meant when he said, "Seek first God's reign and God's justice" (Matthew 6:33). According to Mark and Matthew, Jesus' ministry began with his announcement of the reign of God (Mark 1:14-15 and Matthew 4:12-17). According to Luke, Jesus began his ministry with a message about the Jubilee, based on Isaiah 61:1-2. It is evident that this was Luke's way of explaining the significance of the same message about God's reign (Luke 4:14-30, cf. 4:42-44).

The reign of God that Jesus proclaimed as the Jubilee is clearly an answer to the problem of domination and exclusion; it is a proposal for a world where there is room for all. In the same passage, dealing with his first sermon in the Nazareth synagogue, Jesus offers two examples of God's intervention in history: the case of a widow from Sidon and that of a Syrian man with leprosy. Both were non-Jews; both were doubly or triply marginalized from salvation according to the dominant ideology of the Jews: the man because he was diseased and impure; the widow because she was a woman, a widow, and poor. Luke writes that Jesus' neighbors, who had marveled at his message, were filled with anger upon hearing these examples and tried to kill him—thus anticipating the climax of his ministry—recisely for promoting the Jubilee in favor of the excluded ones.

It is important to read again the whole record of Jesus' ministry and his death and resurrection in light of the Jubilee. We need to see in what ways Jesus not only healed the sick and impure but also identified with them to the point of breaking repeatedly and intentionally the regulations and taboos of the scribes and Pharisees. Both his actions and his words were prophetic and revolutionary to the point of being perceived as a threat to the dominant structures of domination. According to his vision of God's reign and God's justice, women and children, the sick and those possessed by demons, poor and peasants, sinners and impure had priority. And among his followers the first will be last—servants and slaves.

In this rereading of the ministry of Jesus we will look for other signs of the Jubilee, the Sabbath Year, and the Day of Rest, which according to Leviticus 25, Deuteronomy 5 and 15, and Exodus 20 were established by God in order to incarnate among God's people justice and mercy, that is, true spirituality. These mandates were intended to limit and reverse the accumulation of wealth for some and the economic and social marginalization of many in the following ways:

- the remission of debt, which is one of the greatest needs in today's world, for it is through debt that weak persons, social sectors, and whole countries are subjected totally to the exploitation and oppression of the strong
- the liberation of slaves, which today is very closely related to the omnipotence of the market—called free but in fact enslaving—and to the terrible, permanent threat of layoff, resulting in economic, social, and spiritual exclusion
- the redistribution of the land, which in our time represents capital and the essential means for labor, life, identity, and well-being
- rest for all persons, the land, and even the beasts of burden, so that all may have the means of restoring their strength and well-being, and that nature may continue to provide its wealth for the sustenance and reproduction of life for all

We know that the remission of debts appears in the Lord's Prayer (Matthew 6:12), but we do not know how Jesus explained it or how the primitive church understood it. According to Acts 2:43-47 and

4:32-37, the first Christians tried to redistribute their possessions in order to attend to the needy, but we do not know how long they did so. According to 1 Corinthians 11:17-34, the Lord's Supper was to be an expression of unity and solidarity among rich and poor, free and slaves, but it had degenerated into drunkenness and gluttony for some, exclusion and humiliation for others. It had become a negation rather than a realization of the body of Christ. In order to undergird our vision of God's reign and justice we need to reexamine the life of Jesus and that of the primitive church in the light of the Jubilee.

An example of a church that has grasped the centrality of God's reign and God's justice, of inclusion rather than exclusion, and of a world with room for all, is the Unión Evangélica Pentecostal Venezolana. It is an indigenous church, decidedly ecumenical, clearly committed to the poor, and fearlessly prophetic, without minimizing at all its evangelical, charismatic, Pentecostal heritage. At its last assembly, in face of the economic, social, moral, and spiritual devastation that the Venezuelan people are experiencing at this moment in history, this church drew up and published the following "Letter from Guanare" [author's translation]:

> We pastors, delegates of churches, youth organizations, women's societies, children, rural and indigenous sectors, participants at the Thirty-Seventh Convention of the Unión Evangélica Pentecostsal Venezolana, meeting in City of Guanare August 28 to September 1, 1996, wish to share with the people of Venezuela our concerns, hopes, reflections and proposals.
>
> We have been called together under the theme: "Jubilee: Festival of the Spirit," a theme that we consider to be of great relevance to the present reality of Venezuela and Latin America. The Jubilee refers to the festivity celebrated by the Hebrew people and designed to value the land as a community possession, to proclaim the freedom of the slaves, to restore mortgaged lands, to forgive unpayable debts, and reduce to a minimum the economic and social differences accumulated among the people (Leviticus 25).
>
> Recognizing the distance of time, space, and historic development, we affirm that the ethical principles that gave origin to these norms remain in force and constitute a biblical paradigm capable of calling us to the commitment to build a form of social relations founded on justice, solidarity, and peace.

As a church close to the sufferings of the people, we are concerned about the deepening poverty that is occurring as a result of the economic measures that are being applied to our people and that, among other things, manifest our dependence with respect to the center of world power. We have reflected on the weight that the external debt has on the process of impoverishment of our people. Precisely, the biblical paradigm of the Jubilee calls us to pray and work so that the unpayable debts are not transformed into perverse mechanisms that enslave and sacrifice our people on the altars of the creditors.

We call on our government to be honest with the people. They should know that a major part of the money gathered through fiscal measures goes directly into the hands of the international bank. In Venezuela, we have paid in the last ten years 40 billion dollars in service to the debt, and the debt, instead of diminishing, has grown, reaching in 1996, 42 billion dollars. This is translated into the increase in the level of unemployment, the collapse in health services, the raising of prices of basic goods and services, and the general deterioration of the quality of life for the people.

We join the voices of the churches and sectors of good will that call for the realization of an ecumenical Jubilee that will lead to a profound revision of the debt and its remission in the countries that are not able to pay, taking into account that this debt is immoral because it was contracted illegally and behind the backs of the people, who are ultimately the ones who suffer the consequences.

So that this may become a reality, we exhort the peoples and governments of Latin America to work together in the search for a more just international economic order.

Likewise, we also call upon the churches and Christians in general to understand that the clamor for justice for the weak has reached the ears of God. It is necessary that we announce before the world the proclamation of the Year of Grace that Jesus inaugurated at the beginning of his messianic ministry (Luke 4:18-21). That together we bring hope to the people and commit ourselves to pray, work, and orient our people so that we become aware of the challenge that we all have in the face of this great crisis and that we become involved in concrete actions, that they not reduce the Jubilee proposal to mere celebrations and declarations, but that they become effective in the establishment of a greater degree of justice for our people, at the door to the Third Millennium.

Guanare, August 31, 1996

A Vision of Mission:
The Option for and from the Excluded Ones

Facing the challenge of a world where there is room for all, facing Jesus' mandate to seek first God's reign and God's justice, facing the worldwide clamor for full inclusion of the poor, of women, and of black and indigenous peoples, we discover that some of our churches are still exclusive and excluding. Yet, according to current projections, the United States of America will within fifty years have a population that is more than 50 percent non-Anglo.

A church that has not come out of its racial, ethnic, economic, and social captivity will certainly be called into question. This is a matter of identity and integrity in a world increasingly polarized both economically and socially. Churches that are identified with the rich and powerful will find it difficult to struggle for the justice, equality, and well-being of all people—in their local communities, at the national level, and in the world—now that globalization of wealth and poverty face us all directly. But even more fundamentally, this is a matter that has to do with the nature of the gospel and the role of the church in history. It is, above all, a matter of God's nature and of the integrity of God's mission in the world.

Pablo Richard sets forth with wisdom and spirit his option for and from the marginalized and excluded in his article, "Interpretación bíblica desde las culturas indígenas (mayas, kunas y quichuas de América Latina)."[2] Noting that "The Bible was utilized to legitimate the conquest and the destruction of the culture and the religion of the indigenous peoples," Richard traces the imposition, even today, of this culture of domination, not only on indigenous peoples but also on other vulnerable groups. The rationalization of such domination was famously expressed by Juan Gines de Sepulveda in the sixteenth century:

> With perfect rights the Spaniards rule over the barbarians of the New World and adjacent islands, who in terms of prudence,

ingenuity, virtue and humanity are as inferior to the Spaniards as are children to adults and women to men, having among them such difference as that which is found between wild and cruel people and very clement people . . . and I might say monkeys and humans. . . .

Being by nature servants, the barbarians, uncultured and inhuman, fail to admit the domination of those who are more prudent, powerful and perfect than they, domination that would bring them most wonderful utilities, being furthermore a just thing, by natural right, that matter obey form, body the soul, appetite reason, brutes humans, women their husbands, children their parents, imperfection perfection, worse better, for the universal good of all things.[3]

Richard expresses the challenge posed by the globalization of this five hundred-year-old, imperialist culture and ideology—specifically in terms of evangelization and the Bible, both of which were used to legitimize it. At issue is not only the cultural and religious autonomy of indigenous peoples and the humanization of those who dominated them but also a need to recover the integral and liberating message of the Bible itself. This need, in turn, has important implications for the other dimensions of domination that Juan Gines de Sepulveda defends. Richard offers the following analysis:

An interpretation of the Bible from the perspective of Indians, women, the body is therefore a spiritual interpretation carried out with the Spirit with whom it was originally written. The Occidental and colonial reading of the Bible, carried out against Indians, women, the body, is an interpretation that perverts the spiritual sense of the Bible. The Bible was not written with a colonial patriarchal, and anti-corporal spirit but with the Spirit of the poor and oppressed. Therefore only a hermeneutic of liberation can be a hermeneutic of the Spirit, which is the hermeneutic with which the Bible was written.[4]

Therefore indigenous peoples as well as other racial and cultural groups, women, and popular movements have the right and the necessity to resist the impositions of Christendom and to affirm their own spiritual roots. Only in this way will they be able to discover the true message of the Bible and help us all to reconstruct a true spirituality. Thus indigenous peoples, African Americans, women, and other groups excluded from the mainstream, will play an essential role in the recovery of the Bible as a foundation for mission.

The Bible is read and interpreted in the bosom of movements of indigenous and African American peoples, workers and peasants, women, ecologists, and youth. The Word of God is read with the Spirit that becomes visible and active in these movements in relation to the body, culture, women, nature, and youth. The experience of the Spirit is not found in the soul as opposed to the body, but in the affirmation of life over death. Life is affirmed clearly as the fullness of the life of the body, the life of the poor, the Indian, the African American, the woman, youth, and nature. The realm of the Spirit is the world defined as the relationship of body-culture-gender-work-nature. Such an interpretation of the Bible is required by the Spirit. In the popular reading of the Bible, the experience of the Spirit occupies a new social place in history.[5]

On the basis of such an indigenous world vision, we can project a mission that integrates the individual with his or her extended family, community, people, culture, land, environment, and God. We will be able to integrate the experiences, perspectives, and contributions of marginalized groups and reconstruct the mission, the church, theology, the human, the whole creation in accord with the reign of God and God's option for and from the excluded ones.

Not long ago we had a revealing and renewing experience at the Latin American Biblical Seminary. For the last three years we spent long hours and much energy in order to apply for recognition as a university under the National Council of Private Higher Education of Costa Rica. At the same time we increased our involvement in intermediate-level theological studies. We did this because the great majority of pastors and leaders in Latin America are at this level, and they are the ones who lead the churches. The seminary has insufficient human and material resources for a program at this level, but we are preparing study materials for biblical and pastoral institutes of which there are hundreds throughout the region with tens of thousands of students.

Last year we decided to offer at the seminary, in collaboration with the Latin American Evangelical Pentecostal Commission (CEPLA), an intensive month of studies for advanced students, facilitators, and coordinators of these intermediate-level programs. We chose as a general theme, "The Reign of God and the Struggle for Life." The first course was "Latin American Liturgy for Life" and included a workshop for the analysis and creation of hymns and choruses. The second course, "The Book of Revelation and the

Struggle for Life in Latin America," was led by a Pentecostal bishop. During the third week the main course, "Barriers for None: Ministry with Differently Abled People," was directed by a blind Baptist pastor from Cuba and a quadriplegic layman from Nicaragua. The final course, "The Biblical Jubilee and the Struggle for Life," integrated all these with the general theme. Thirty-one pastors and leaders participated in the event, all of them educators and students who were open and cooperative, overcoming enormous theological and ideological prejudices, creating intense community within their wide diversity, and demonstrating that we can open important doors within the evangelical movement to the struggle for life in Latin America. They were an inspiration for the whole seminary community.

Conclusion

The vision of mission proposed here may differ greatly from that of our predecessors. When we consider the history of the first conquest of Latin America 500 years ago, accompanied by Catholic missionaries, and the second conquest beginning 150 years ago, accompanied by Protestant missionaries, we recognize that God's mission cannot be limited to personal evangelism and the planting of churches. When we consider the history of Latin America since the Panama Congress of 1916, we recognize that God's mission cannot be limited to the multiplication of missions and the growth of Protestant and Pentecostal churches. When we consider the systems of domination that determine the life and death, the dignity and well-being of the Latin American peoples, we must broaden our vision of mission. If we recognize that the purpose of God's mission is to create a world where there is room for all and that God's reign, by definition, brings justice and shalom for all, we must invite all the members of our churches to join hands with all our peoples, with the diverse liberation and human-rights movements, with representatives of all social sectors, and with other religious and cultural groups, beginning with our common struggle for survival and moving on to seek fullness of life and dignity for all, even for all creation.

This vision may call for difficult changes for our members, for missionaries, and for the congregations that have traditionally sent and supported these missionaries. The old missionary mentality suffered from a messianic syndrome because it was convinced that it had the last and complete word of salvation and because it was so deeply involved in propagating that message. We can and must learn from the mission of Jesus, for it was the little ones and the sinners, the marginalized and the despised, not the righteous and the important, the strong and the sure, who received the reign of God. So, too, said Paul, the great missionary to the Gentiles.

Faced with the pessimism and hopelessness of many, on the one hand, and the triumphalism of the new missionary movements, on the other, God may be calling us to a different way with a new vision of the world, of God's reign, and of our mission. We can celebrate the fact that at the end of the second millennium hardly a society remains in which there is not a growing recognition of the rights of women, the poor, all racial and cultural groups, those differently abled—all people and all creation. Our Latin American reading of the gospel of Jesus Christ impels us to celebrate the irruption of God's reign on all these frontiers in our churches and societies, in both the North and the South.

End Notes
1. Walter Wink, *Engaging the Powers: Discernment and Resistance in a World of Domination*, (Minneapolis: Augsburg Fortress Publishers, 1992) p. 51.
2. Pablo Richard, "Interpretación bíblica desde las culturas indígenas (mayas, kunas y quichuas de América Latina)," *Pasos*, no. 66 (July-August), 1996.
3. Ibid.
4. Ibid.
5. Ibid.

Religious Pluralism and the Emergence of the Excluded: Challenges to Ecumenism and Mission in Latin America

Walter Altmann

Walter Altmann, professor of systematic theology at São Leopoldo Theological Seminary, Rio Grande do Sul, Brazil, is president of the Latin American Council of Churches.

How much has changed in the understanding of ecumenism and mission during this last century! In 1910, at the International Conference on Mission in Edinburgh, the organizers thought they could exclude Latin America because the region was already entirely Christian. In 1963, at the World Conference on Mission and Evangelism in Mexico City—a conference that I had the privilege of attending as a youth delegate from Brazil—there was recognition of the need for "mission on six continents." Now, as we approach the end of the century, delegates to the 1996 World Conference on Mission and Evangelism in Salvador (Bahia), Brazil, met with the intention of seeking to understand and celebrate the gospel in different cultures.

At the dawn of a new millennium we ask ourselves about the present situation and about the prospects for a program of unity and mission among Christians and Latin Americans of other faiths. John's admonition, "that they may all be one" (John 17:21), is for the churches a biblical mandate to seek unity, but it is a mandate based on the gift of unity that already existed between Jesus and the Father, a gift through which Jesus intercedes on behalf of his disciples before his death. There is a missiological dimension, as well: "so that the world may believe."

This essay will focus specifically on the theme of ecumenism and mission in Latin America, and it will do so from two distinct perspectives: religious pluralism and the emergence of new social subjects. There are two ways of dealing with our theme, one using a descriptive and analytical focus of the current religious situation and the other using a more biblical and theological evaluation of the significance of the poor and the excluded.

The Growth of Religious Pluralism in Latin America

The religious scene in Latin America and the Caribbean is currently one of intense mobility and growing diversity. For many centuries, Latin America was considered to be a homogeneous region, at least in religious terms. Here "homogeneous" meant Catholic. Today, the region is increasingly defined by its religious pluralism. On the one hand, the growth of some Pentecostal movements, particularly the neo-Pentecostal movement, is truly astounding, and their expressions of faith are embraced with great fervor by vast multitudes. On the other hand, we can observe another process developing more silently but with profound implications. That is the rediscovery of the religious expressions of indigenous and African communities that were previously practiced clandestinely without the general knowledge or interest of the larger society, at times, certainly, to avoid persecution on religious grounds.

The reasons for this mobility and diversity, of course, are multiple: They stem from the lack of certainty about the future, from the emptiness of a Christian catechism that is often little more than a formality, and from a routine, repetitious expression of Christian faith. They stem, also, from the suffering caused by social exclusion—an exclusion that is particularly acute in the field of health care. The change from religious adherence to a traditional faith seen as empty to acceptance of new expressions of religious faith is invariably accompanied by the sensation of discovering something new, a rediscovery of values that have been repressed. This new form of faith not only provides a sense of being valued as a person but also establishes specific forms of fraternal community relationships in the midst of an anonymous metropolis where so many rural migrants have been displaced.

It is also true that historical memory flourishes in times of religious tolerance. It cannot be forgotten that the original Christian faith brought to this region was not embraced as a result of of simple persuasion but in large part through coercion. As such, it was not respectful of traditional values among indigenous peoples or among the enslaved black populations. It is also true that—thank God!—not everything was done through coercion. There was also mission in solidarity with indigenous populations and the poor in general.

Nevertheless, the predominant pattern was an alliance between the throne and the altar, along with, later, the connection of Protestant missions with foreign models of modernity. It is not coincidence that there is today a notable resurgence of traditional indigenous and African religious expressions in Latin America and the Caribbean. We can no longer regard this process as an isolated phenomenon. Rather, it is a general trend observable throughout the continent. For example, among the Mayans in Guatemala, the indigenous populations in Chiapas, the Quechuas and the Aymaras in the Andean region, and among blacks in Brazil and Cuba. It is the reaffirmation of an identity that has been suppressed for a long, long time. In the last few years there has also been a noticeable attraction of indigenous communities for evangelical churches, particularly Pentecostal churches—an attraction that may be attributed largely to the fact that these churches allow a form of community affirmation in the face of deteriorating living conditions in the society, rather than solely to proselytism or questionable practices on the part of these churches.

These observations should not diminish in any way the criticism that can or even should be made of so-called "evangelical" religious practices that are likely to violate cultural or social values of indigenous and African communities, as traditional Christian religious expression has done. But it is certainly true that indigenous communities and African-Latin American and Caribbean peoples are no longer permitting outside forces to tell them what to do. Rather, they are making use of their own ability to decide, among other things, their choice of religious practice. And they are doing it in a pluralistic manner. That is, they are intentionally turning to Catholic religious expression or opting for the "evangelical alternative" or seeking to recover the religious expression of their ancestors.

Among the reasons for the surge of new religious movements — some of them drawn from Oriental spirituality—it is just as important to mention the "spiritual fatigue" found in modern Western rationalism. There seems no escape from the chilliness of the view that we have reached the "end of utopias" on earth. Added to all of this is the mystique of the approaching end not only of a century but of a millennium. A thousand years ago, at the end of the first millennium after Christ, there was a spectacular explosion of apocalyptic expectations.

No doubt the scene is set for religious expressions based on naive credibility; leaders are often unscrupulous and take advantage of the prevailing sense of anxiety and eternity to make a quick profit. Such leaders may, on the one hand, include extortioners and other charlatans—particularly those with promises of "divine healing." They may, on the other hand, include those who use more subtle ways to spread, in the evangelical setting, a theology of prosperity that promises to the faithful (and those who contribute the full tithe) all sorts of "blessings." They may promise miraculous financial compensation, which appeals strongly to those who want to leave behind the bitter present.

It would be totally simplistic, nevertheless, to attribute the growth of new religious expressions entirely to the opportunism of corrupt leaders, or, worse yet, to the ignorance of the population. There is, underlying all of this growth, the unfailing dedication of countless popular religious leaders who are rediscovering themselves as active agents of social change. They and their followers are discovering meaning and faith, lives transformed from abandon to disciplined direction, and noticeable improvement, even if limited, of the quality of life for the individual or family—all at the heart of a community of faith. This experience is the cornerstone of the characteristic fervor of the new evangelical and Pentecostal religiosity.

The Ecumenical Challenge in Latin American Religious Pluralism

There are no signs to indicate that the trend toward religious pluralism might in some way be reversed over the coming years. To the contrary, everything leads us to believe that the process will intensify. All indications are that Latin America and the Hispanic Caribbean will, in the future, be an even more colorful spectrum of plurality than it is today. Or, to say it more directly, the continent will, in the future, be less Catholic, and more Pentecostal. Furthermore, it will have significant space for indigenous and African religious expression, as well as a real presence, however modest, of historic Protestantism.[1]

There is no doubt that this situation is seen by many traditional churches as threatening. Historic Protestantism is "trapped" between the great Roman Catholic Church and the phenomenon of Pentecostal growth; it must undertake a radical questioning about its own identity, or it could even be forced into a struggle for its own survival. There are some exceptions, it is true, in which historic Protestantism has known how to tune into the deepest yearnings of the people and their struggles. But these exceptions seem to confirm the rule. We can not hide from the fact that although historic Protestantism grew in the past, there are now unmistakable signs that it may be "lost" or out of touch with the new heartbeat of the times. Under such a threat, the biggest temptation for Protestantism is capitulation, that is, the attempt to imitate Pentecostalism, adopting its spirituality as well as its forms of preaching and worshiping. On the one hand, such imitation is doomed to fail because of Protestantism's inability to do it as well as the Pentecostal churches. Furthermore, such adaptation would represent a renunciation of the specific ecumenical contributions that Protestant churches should be making: the permanent and rigorous reliance on biblical criteria as indispensable for all ecclesiastical practices; the constant reference to the cross of Christ as an evangelical perspective in the face of various "enthusiasms," often ephemeral and illusory; and the openness for renewal based on the experience and practices of other churches. On the other hand, the most painful part for Protestantism, as it debates its own identity and survival, will certainly be having to define its missionary task in a clearly ecumenical sense, giving first priority to evangelical integrity rather than giving in to the compulsion of denominational growth.

It is understandable that the Catholic Church may feel particularly threatened by the intense religious mobility because it has always seen itself, whether officially or not, as the religion of the Latin American peoples, not just one religious expression among others. Even today, the overwhelming majority of people in Latin America profess to be Catholic. The arrival in Latin America of historic Protestantism, especially during the second half of the last century and the first half of this one, was a shock for the Catholic Church, particularly when these new groups reached into the upper, more educated sectors of society. But these challenges were nothing in comparison to the current Pentecostal wave, which is washing away, so to speak, large portions of the population. Even the relationship toward the emerging indigenous and African religious expressions harbors the expectation of syncretic assimilation. Assimilation is not likely, however, with Pentecostalism, which is frequently militantly anti-Catholic. Confronted by this unusual religious pluralism, the temptation for the Catholic Church may be to yearn for the return of the "good old days" of union with the power of the state or at least to a return of social privileges guaranteed by the state—for example, religious teaching in the public schools. Nevertheless, a significant ecumenical contribution, which only Catholicism can provide, is the sense of universality and unity in the sacraments. However, this contribution may be acceptable only if, in the current context, it is accompanied by unmistakable signs—a painful process, to be sure—of the recognition of the legitimacy of different religious options in Latin America. Moreover, we must not forget how profoundly significant for the rest of the churches the renewal of Catholicism, as experienced in the last few decades, has been. One need consider only the widespread movement of grassroots (base) Christian communities which unite the experience of faith and spirituality with a significant practice of community and social action.

The Pentecostal churches, which have been, until now, the grand beneficiaries of the growing religious pluralism, and whose mobility has given them such rapid growth, are showing signs that they, too, are beginning to feel the negative effects of stiff religious competition. For them, too, religious pluralism is no longer just an opportunity but is also seen as a threat. Furthermore, these new religious movements are experiencing the problems of "the second generation," that is to say, of how to proceed when the novelty has worn off and the situations are more complex than were imagined during the initial enthusiasm. It is precisely these situations, however, that can reinforce the most significant positive contribution that the Pentecostal churches are making and surely will continue to make: to be an expression of "pentecostalness" (as Bernardo Campos phrases it) that is, of the freedom and dynamism of the Spirit in an era of intense spiritual quest and social mobility. At the same time, Pentecostalism's temptation seems to be the sharpening of "religious confrontations" by means of ever more intense competition, a dangerous and total contradiction of the biblical mandate for unity. Even though Pentecostal churches, in general, view the term ecumenical with great suspicion (often the result of misunderstandings that can be resolved), the necessary *ecumenical* step—one of hope as well as pain—consists of the gradual recognition of historic Protestants and of Catholics as brothers and sisters in Christ, precisely because of the freedom of the Holy Spirit itself. True "pentecostalness" is much broader than various confessional expressions.

The equally notable resurgence of African and indigenous religious expression is in part the fruit of the increased awareness in 1992 of the five hundredth anniversary of the arrival of the European invaders and occupiers of the New World. Bringing with them a culture and religion that they considered to be superior, they imposed it on the original peoples of these lands and on those who had been forcibly brought as slaves. Although the religious expression of all these cultures was suppressed for centuries, it survived, often clandestinely or by resorting to forms of religious syncretism. It now reemerges with its own identity in a new context of pluralism, affirming itself in the face of—or even against— Christianity, which it regards, with good reason, as an integral part of the dominant culture.

All this religious turbulence certainly presents a tremendous challenge for Christians, and it offers an opportunity for repentance and calls for a new way of behaving. The phenomenon calls attention to the "irreducibleness of the other" and the fact that Christ is found in the other—particularly in those who are marginalized (Matthew 25:31-46). God is not limited to the borders of Christianity. His spirit will act wherever it chooses. For Catholicism, its traditional stance of superiority toward indigenous and African religious expression is apparently, and necessarily, being revised in the sense that it can allow the incorporation or even the gradual syncretistic assimilation of concepts and diverse religious practices under its strong hierarchical and sacramental unity. Protestantism, which is much more centered on doctrinal fidelity, resists syncretism and assimilation. Still, let us not forget that correct doctrine, rather than a magical formula, is the confessional expression of the reality of God's love. Yet, the important thing is this reality, not the doctrine itself. What historical Protestantism could do well, would be to develop, based on confessional and biblical premises, a position of full respect and a radical sense of legitimacy for diverse expressions of religion, seeking encounter and dialogue and the affirmation of life in the midst of multiple forms of social and cultural exclusion.

This possibility of encounter and dialogue instead of confrontation and cultural violence is, unfortunately, still far beyond the conceptual horizon or actual experience of many evangelical communities, both historical Protestants and Pentecostals. While the indigenous and African groups are trying to recover or reaffirm their own ethnic, cultural, and religious identity, churches in general view these movements with much suspicion and prejudice. We frequently hear such terms as "superstition," "witchcraft," and "idolatry." Since the recovery of African or indigenous identity is accompanied, quite understandably, by a sharp reaction against the violence of the white invasion over the last five hundred years, the potential risk of an acute religious confrontation cannot be written off. Such a confrontation would surely involve and seriously affect the more populous and poorer sectors of the Latin America peoples.[2]

What Is Our Ecumenical Task?

Thus, there is not the least doubt that the eminent challenge is ecumenical dialogue and cooperation, among the churches and among different religious expressions. We have to consider, as well, that, in a certain way, the reality of increasing religious pluralism corresponds to the evolution of the economy—like a mirror, in which the "religious marketplace" is also a reflection of the globalized economic marketplace. In this way, religious pluralism also suffers from what can be called a "warped coherence," since each religious expression claims to be an integrating force, bringing together all dimensions of life, providing faith and meaning, giving guidance and hope, enabling the practice of solidarity and justice. To avoid falling into mutual conflict, if not new forms of "holy wars" or all-out competition, the only biblical and theologically responsible option is that of ecumenical dialogue and cooperation.

Fortunately, throughout the length and breadth of Latin America there are many fundamental ecumenical experiences and initiatives that could be strengthened: weeks of prayer for unity; Bible study groups; ecumenical consultations and courses; training courses for pastoral agents; and cooperation on issues of economic development, health care, education, peace, defense of human rights, justice, and preservation of nature. Much more can be done in the production of ecumenical materials for mutual understanding without prejudice and of other catechetical materials for ecumenical religious teaching as well as for public statements by the churches on pertinent social, political, and economic issues. It is customary for followers of different religious expressions to find one another and cooperate significantly when facing needs and specific challenges: the struggle of peasant and indigenous peoples for land, the care for nature, the quest for peace with justice, defense of the dignity of life, and other important issues.

On an institutional level, organizations such as the World Council of Churches (WCC), Latin American Council of Churches (CLAI), National Council of the Churches of Christ in the USA (NCCCUSA),

Latin American Episcopal Conference [Roman Catholic] (CELAM), Latin American Theological Fraternity (LTF), and other organizations could deepen their fraternal contacts. To give just one example: in Central America, the Roman Catholic Church, on the one hand, and the ecumenical councils, on the other, made significant contributions to the peace process. They could, however, have done so in a more closely coordinated, perhaps even more effective manner. Such joint action may be extremely important in the development and execution of further education for peace and justice.

Furthermore, as we have seen, the ecumenical challenge extends beyond the relationships among Christian churches and embraces religious expressions in a much broader sense. The common ground necessary for encounter and dialogue, in a region of such suffering as Latin America and the Caribbean, is in my view found in the affirmation and dignity of life as a gift of God. With this phrase, I am by no means advocating syncretism at all levels but, rather, defending the need for full respect of our differences and the freedom to choose our own religious option as an affirmation of life. Unfortunately, however, this vision is held by only a small minority of churches. One step in this direction could be the development of a general awareness that religious expression entails profound and deeply personal convictions and their manifestations in community, and that one faith should never impose itself by coercive means but, rather, should be accepted and developed in freedom.

Lastly, we should remember that poverty and social injustice, heightened in recent years by neoliberal economic programs and the resulting exclusion of many segments of the population, continue to challenge the effective practice of Christian solidarity. This solidarity cannot be made real in a divided manner without a serious loss of effectiveness and credibility. The same is true for the continuation of the peace process in several Latin American countries. We should recall that, even though political and social violence has decreased in some countries, a significant number of Christians, both laity and clergy, including both Protestant and Pentecostal pastors, have in recent years suffered violence and death in several countries including Guatemala, Mexico, Colombia, and Peru. It is clear that those who are in power continue to regard such faith as a threat and try to suppress it. If the weak and the poor did not hold on to hope —and the strength that such hope can unleash—violence by those in power might not manifest itself in such harsh ways. Instead, it could be maintained behind the scenes. Nevertheless, it is precisely in this violent reaction by those in power that we can perceive the continuing effectiveness of hope and a definitive victory for faith, even though throughout history it has always come under threat.

Theological and Missiological Challenges Through the Emergence of the Excluded

In speaking about the emergence of the excluded, I have in mind what Gustavo Gutierrez and others have called "the irruption of the poor." We must recognize that today, the expression "the poor" is perceived as either too generalized, hiding the real faces of the poor, or else as a concept that reduces everything to the economic factor and discards other equally vital aspects. But let us not get ahead of ourselves. I suggest that we first look back to the time when "the poor" occupied center stage in theology and church practice in Latin America. Although the poor have never been absent from history, in the 1960s they took a central place, and practice combined the lived experience of faith with a search for social transformation. Through the formation of base communities, this combination resulted in a theology of liberation. It also created a prophetic church in solidarity, a voice for those who have no voice. During the dark decades of military dictatorships, it was a significant channel for resistance by the peoples of Latin America.[3]

Countless people throughout Latin America tried to live out "the identification with the poor," sometimes in spectacular ways, more often anonymously in the small gestures of everyday life. It was a way of life that sought to reflect, in a clear and radical way, the life and practice of Jesus. And yet the concept of identification with the poor revealed its limitations, and it became evident that an even more radical process was called for: the irruption of the poor themselves. Here the process points in the other direction. No longer do the representatives of the center, of the norm, of power, break down the barriers of discrimination and oppression in order to be in solidarity with the poor, the victims of the system. Rather, it is the victims themselves who, through a radical awakening of their own consciousness, recognize their own identities and tear down the limits that have confined them, asking questions, determining their own discourse, and demanding their right to transform reality. It is here that they also reaffirm or recover their culture and, with that, their traditional religion.

There is another sense in which the appellation "the poor" was seen, in the end, as limited. As a generic concept it allowed the real faces of the poor to be hidden from view. This was, in fact, one of the criticisms increasingly leveled against proponents of liberation theology: they were not clearly naming "the poor," and by adopting a dominant or even exclusive socioeconomic perspective as the dominant or even exclusive factor, they were setting aside other groups that suffered just as much discrimination, marginalization, and oppression, such as, for example, blacks and women. The debates that developed within the various currents of liberation theology—Latin American, black, feminist, and others—were at times harsh and filled with emotion and mutual accusation. Nevertheless, they brought increased maturity and greater dignity to Latin America's theology of liberation. There was a general recognition that the criticism was, at its core, pertinent, even though in some areas there continued to be resistance. Because of this acceptance, theological work in Latin America is being enriched.

As a result of these searing debates, there is today a much clearer perception of the irruption of the poor. They are perceived as people with individual faces and proper identities: women, indigenous peoples, or blacks. Moreover, they reflect not only various forms of oppression, but represent specific groups that have emerged as important social players on their own: landless peasants, the homeless, the unemployed, street children, women thrown into prostitution. The list could continue almost indefinitely. All these groups and their activities for social justice and recognition constitute, as they become visible and make themselves heard, the irruption of the poor—or of the excluded, as we prefer to call them today.

And what does this irruption of the excluded have to do with the mission of the churches? We spoke before about a radical reversal: from being objects of a history made by others—the dominators— the excluded have burst forth and become the subjects of their own history. Can we also foresee a similar reversal in the mission of the church? In what sense are the excluded becoming the evangelizers and the nonexcluded the evangelized?[4]

The Excluded as Evangelizers

To seek theological responses to this question, one might try returning to the parable of the judgment of the sheep and the goats (Matthew 25:31-46).[5] How do these brothers and sisters, these littlest ones, become the presence, grace and challenge of Christ for us? This parable has caused difficulties for Protestant interpreters because it seems to contradict the doctrine of justification by grace and faith. The sheep and the goats will be judged by what they did or did not do for these persons who are little brothers and sisters of Jesus. To enter the kingdom will be the reward, and to be thrown out will be the punishment.

But there is no contradiction. In truth, the final judgment is preceded by grace. "When you did this for the least of them, you did it to me," says Jesus. "When you did not do these things for the littlest of my small ones, it was to me that you did not do it." Jesus is already encountering all of us in the person of the littlest of these. One may object, but in the parable, the persons who are set aside on the right and the left of the king and judge did not know that Jesus would be found among the needy persons mentioned. They were surprised by the argument of the judge and asked, "Lord, when did we do this to you? Or "when did we see you and not do this for you?" Nevertheless, after Jesus has told us this story, we cannot ignore it. Jesus is to be found in the needy persons, his little brothers and sisters.

Jesus' story means that the excluded ones are a twofold manifestation of God's grace: as consolation and as challenge. Because Jesus identifies himself with them, the excluded can experience grace themselves. That is good news for them, their consolation. Furthermore, because Jesus identifies himself with them, they become transformed by grace for those who are not excluded; that is, the nonexcluded can recognize Christ in the excluded and thus are confronted with the challenges of Jesus. Jesus' identification, then, is simultaneously the good news and a challenge. How are those who are not excluded going to relate to those who are? With an attitude of disdain, superiority, discrimination, and oppression? If so, grace will be their condemnation ("to me you have left this undone"). Or in a spirit of reconciliation, solidarity, peace, and justice? If so, grace, as the creative word of God, becomes the basis for new relationships among persons, communities, and the larger society ("you have done this to me").

Either way, from Christ and through Christ, the excluded are the "evangelizers." Not because of what they do—their merits, to use traditional theological language—but because of who they are in their destitute condition, a condition through which they place a demand on us with a dignity that is conferred on them by God. It is because of this condition, and only this, that there are no excluded ones among them. In other words, these evangelizers are not only the "good" excluded, whose consciousness has been raised and who are organized (once again, the term "good" is, of course, defined by the nonexcluded!), but, rather, all of the excluded, without exception. They are called by the immeasurable grace of God, who unlike us, does not exclude anyone.

Resurrection in the Midst of the Reality of Death

To the necessary statement just made should be added, with just as much emphasis, the statement that Jesus is identified with the excluded not so that they will remain forever in their situation of destitution and oppression, but, rather, so that they will no longer be cursed, so that they can come forth as new actors in the history that is being laid out by the nonexcluded. Certainly there is a perspective of resurrection after death. Or better yet: by means of the presence and grace of Christ, his resurrection has started in the midst of the conditions of death. The kingdom is already becoming reality. Thus, the nonexcluded who have experienced grace from the situation of the excluded, reconciling themselves and coming into solidarity with them, can now accept the challenge that has been posed to them by this grace. They may become "the poor in spirit" (Matthew 5:3) and place themselves decidedly on the side of the poor and the excluded, walking by their side, taking as their own the anguish and the hopes of the excluded. In a sense, also, they will experience resurrection in the midst of death. The kingdom is already among them.

Death and resurrection—how close they can be to each other! In July 1996 I participated on behalf of CLAI in a pastoral visit by ecumenical councils to Colombia. When we divided into small groups to visit different regions of the country, I traveled with Jane Sullivan, who represented the National Council of Churches in the USA. We went to Uraba, an area that has suffered the highest levels of violence in that country. The local person assigned to organize our visit was the Reverend Isai Perez, a Presbyterian pastor who, in February 1997, was "invited" by armed men to leave the region with his family in twenty-four hours. Who can reproach him for complying with such an order? Only three months earlier, the Presbyterian pastor Pedro Alzate, a peasant who had participated in our ecumenical activities, was ordered off a bus and executed on the spot in front of members of his congregation who were traveling with him.

There is not greater love than this: "To lay down one's life for one's friends" (John 15:13). The struggles that continue to emerge, and the continuing challenges of discipleship and mission may have as a consequence the laying down of one's life. But, we confess in our faith, whoever "loses" life in this way has "saved it" and has gone from death to life. Pedro Alzate, whose face Jane and I still see before us, has his name written in the book of life. He has completed God's mission.

End Notes

1. Some observations about the categories being used here, which are problematic, up to a point, but nevertheless, still necessary. The problem comes from the fact that the diversity is so great among religious expressions that one can not truly reduce them to only three or four types without losing important specificities. For example: where is the necessary distinction between Pentecostalism and neo-Pentecostalism? And where does one place Anglicanism, which is both Catholic and Protestant? It is also a problem because one type of spirituality or religious movement can be found within other forms of expressions. For example: the Pentecostal expressions are growing within historical Protestant churches, as well as within Catholicism. We can find the "other" is also significantly within ourselves. At the same time, a large number of Pentecostals see themselves as a movement within Protestantism, and do not want to be excluded from it by the analysis made by other Protestants. Likewise, there is a "catholic memory" within Protestantism. It is known that the reformers did not intend to create new churches. And the inverse is also true, there has been an "evangelical irruption" within Catholicism, in a noticeable manner, during Vatican Council II. Inside Pentecostalism, one can find a growing openness for the ecumenical, even though many—and perhaps the majority still—prefer to believe in the idea of "growth by division," as one person affirmed to me with great candor.

   Nevertheless, the categories are necessary for at least two reasons. One reason has to do with the historical effects of a movement, oftentimes not coinciding with the intentions of the original founder. Luther, for example, tried to renew the church by means of the word; nevertheless, by historical circumstances, Lutheranism emerged as a distinct new faith. In a way, his success produced a historical effect that extended beyond what he intended. Likewise, one can say that the expansion of Pentecostalism broke down the barriers of Protestantism and acquired the right to its own identity. The second reason for using these categories is purely pragmatic and pedagogical: they try to capture the nature and essential characteristics of a diversified moment. It is in this sense that we are using these categories, fully aware of their limitations and precariousness, as well as of the intercommunication and mutual influences that exist among diverse expressions.

2. I dare to make this observation, even though it may appear to be a reflection of a "white man's" concern in the face of legitimate claims of indigenous and African communities crying out against centuries of oppression. Therefore, this observation will only be pertinent in the measure that it is also accompanied by clear signs—from the Christian side— of effective repentance from a history of ethnic and cultural oppression.

3. The genesis and development of a theology and practice of liberation are associated mostly, or even exclusively with the Catholic Church. There is no doubt that the renewal of the Catholic Church during those years meant an extraordinary ecumenical contribution to the mission of other churches. We are indebted to this renewal. And yet, we need to remember that when the awareness and practice of liberation first appeared, it was an ecumenical phenomenon, not at all limited to the Catholic Church. During those years,

many Protestants were deeply involved during those years in ecumenical initiatives, such as student movements or social actions, and inside their own churches they were also part of profound efforts for renewal. There was an intense social concern and a search for the significance of the gospel and faith in Christ to respond to the reality of oppression in Latin America: organizations such as Church and Society in Latin America (ISAL), the Latin American Council of Churches (CLAI), the Committee for Cooperation with Latin America (CCLA), and many others have their roots largely in this concern and search and this spirit.

Many people who participated in these processes suffered discrimination and even persecution in their own churches. The political conditions forced a good number of them to flee into exile, or to become casualties under the terrifying category of "disappeared," like Mauricio Lopez in Argentina. Other persons had less bitter days and were able to contribute to their churches by becoming more committed and being in solidarity with those who were suffering under the secular structures of oppression. Churches began to raise their voices and to act on issues of land tenure, human rights, and the cause of indigenous peoples (just to mention a few examples). There was also, in the end, the participation of Christians in the revolutionary process, such as in Nicaragua. All of this effort helped to create a Protestantism that was more in solidarity, even though, because of its smallness in size, it never became the outlet for the popular masses. But it was the leaven in many places. (In this context, it is only fair to remember the highly significant contributions made by Richard Shaull, a North American theologian who lived for many decades in Latin America and inspired many Latin American Protestants.)

The spirit that motivated these movements was "the poor," or rather, the identification with the poor. As an example of what it meant concretely and existentially to live this identification with the poor, I am reminded of Roberto and Lori, who as theology students became interested in the indigenous cause and went on to become the first Brazilian Lutheran missionaries among the Indians. They went as missionaries to share in the life of the indigenous peoples of the Amazon, first among the Suruis, from where they were expelled by the government agency responsible for protecting the Indians, but did not like the type of solidarity being adopted by Lori and Roberto. Nor did the agency like being denounced for the arbitrariness committed by government functionaries against the Indians. Lori and Roberto went then to live among the Kulinas, in a village that could only be reached after several days travel by boat. They remained there for several years. When they were expecting their second child, they resolved to renounce the comforts and resources of a hospital, far from the village, because they understood that it would compromise their solidarity. Later, Lori wrote an impressive description of how enriching it had been to bring her child to life there, in the village, surrounded by the love, care, and wisdom of the indigenous women.

4. Or to ask the question in another manner: assuming that from the point of view of the Christian, mission consists in the coming of Christ, then in what way does the person who is economically poor constitute for me, as a member of the middle class, the presence, grace, and challenge of Christ? In what sense are women (or more specifically, my wife, Madalena) becoming for me as a male, the presence, grace, and challenge of Christ? In what sense does the indigenous, the black, become for me, as a white Brazilian of German ancestry, the presence, grace, and challenge of Christ? In what sense does the child in the streets become for me—an adult with a home to live in—the presence, grace and challenge of Christ? In what sense does a small country like Cuba become for the rest of Latin America and the Caribbean, and above all to the powerful giant in the north, the presence, grace and challenge of Christ? The list continues . . . .

5. Although using now generically the expression of "the poor" or of "the excluded," we should keep in mind that the expression is not to be understood as an abstract concept, but rather referring to specific faces already listed in the previous sections. In the parable, Jesus has also started "concretely with the excluded," and not with a generic term: He identifies the persons who are hungry, thirsty, strangers in the land, the naked, the sick, those in prison. Later, Jesus does use a more generic term, as well, namely, "my brothers and sisters, the littlest of these."

Three Biblical Reflections for Our Time

Elsa Tamez

Elsa Tamez received her doctorate from the University of Lausanne, Switzerland. She is dean and professor of theology at the Latin American Biblical Seminary in San José, Costa Rica.

We live in a world of injustice—in a time that the author compares to a house of horrors. These reflections on three books of the Bible—Job, 1 Peter, and Galatians—offer insights about how to live responsible lives that are connected with all of God's people.

Of Silence and of Crying Out (Job)

In June 1995, as a friend and I were walking through a park near the White House, in Washington, D.C., we saw a green tent standing all alone on a lawn, a considerable distance from the path. I asked my friend what it was. She replied that she thought it was someone on a hunger strike.

Her answer made a deep impression on me. In the loneliness of that small green tent someone was perhaps trying to call attention to an injustice. But no one approached, even out of curiosity. I felt that the silence in that space was a shout, but nobody was listening. People were distant, distracted, thinking, perhaps, about the latest gadgets on the market, or their personal problems, or their careers. Nearby was the wall announcing on its fine marble the 50,000 petrified names of youth who had died in Vietnam. All the passion of the struggle over that war seemed to have become a display of antiques.

The scene reminded me of a strike in Costa Rica by teachers who were demanding their pensions and who met total failure. Such painstaking efforts, so much struggle, leading to nothing, except, perhaps, the loss of their jobs.

The churches and Christians in general are being faced everywhere with the problems of exclusion, insensitivity, and lack of solidarity—in direct opposition to the message of Jesus Christ. We live in a time of increasing dehumanization, not only of the excluded but of everyone.

From the garbage dump we hear the voice of Job: "I cry out, 'violence', and no one answers me; I ask for help and no one defends me" (19:7). Here is someone who cries out, asking for justice, demanding an explanation for unjust suffering. The strikers in Costa Rica and the silent protester in Washington cried out in a way, and there was no answer. Today, the majority of the excluded in large cities do not shout; some cry out softly, seeming to know in advance that they will not be heard. They are there working at the garbage dump, gathering, breathing, smelling, eating, touching, asking for trash. Perhaps they don't cry out because those who pass by are wearing earphones and cannot hear them.

Can Job teach us anything for our own day? The garbage dump, though much larger, is still much the same as in his time, even if the actions of the characters are different. There are today Jobs who do not cry out, there are no friends like Job's that attack you in order to defend God, and the absence of the Almighty is unbearably postponed. In this biblical reflection on Job, I want to discuss the silences, the cries, and the grace of God.

The Silences

In the book of Job we find various kinds of silences. Some come out of a deep sense of communion, some are desired, some are devastating. The first and most intense is one that lasts for seven days and seven nights. Three friends, Eliphaz, Bildad, and Zophar, "set out from their place" and went to see him and "share his pain and console him" (2:11). The narrator tells us that when they recognized Job from a distance, "they wept aloud, tore their robes and threw dust over their heads and in the air, and they stayed there with him, sitting on the ground for seven days and nights, without saying a word, seeing how great was his suffering" (2:12-13).

This silence was lived in the space of him who suffered. The text tells us that his friends left their homes and went to see him. They stopped at Job's new home, the dump and found him sitting on the ground in the midst of the garbage. They were scandalized when they saw the repugnant body. Any spoken word at that moment would have been useless.

The silence was the greater part of wisdom. This was the silence of solidarity that tunes in and harmonizes with the souls, the tears, and the rhythms of the heart. The only discordant sound was made by Job, using the potsherd to scrape his loathsome sores (2:8). Job later pleads for the wisdom of silence, but it is not repeated. The rest of the book consists of discourse built on reason. Rational discourse will complicate the friendships and destroy solidarity.

Wisdom at that moment lay not in employing reason to explore the causes of suffering, but, rather, in engaging the five senses to be moved to compassion. The friends saw, heard, smelled, and touched, and they tasted their own tears. They lived the silence of solidarity, intense and moving—a silence that can humanize and bring communion. To be moved when faced with the misfortune of another implies recognition of the other as a human being, and it is a sign of one's own humanity. It is a process of mutual humanization.

There is a second kind of silence—a silence that instructs. Job asks repeatedly that his friends, the wise, be quiet and listen: "Listen carefully to my words, and let this be your consolation; be patient while I speak" (21:2-3). The friends talk and talk and yet are not able to listen to arguments that are contrary to tradition. The reality of suffering by the innocent does not destroy their beliefs. They prefer to defend their mental framework, thinking that they are defending God. Job tells them "I wish to God that you would be completely silent, that would be your wisdom! Please listen to my arguments, pay attention the reasoning of my lips. Your warnings are dusty proverbs, and your replies are of clay. . . Listen carefully to my words, lend your ears to my discourse" (13:5-17). Furthermore, Job is willing to keep silent in order to hear new arguments that can explain the injustice. He asks to be taught and promises to keep silence while the others expound on their wisdom (6:24). These are the active silences—of listening and of openness to change. Job feels that nobody listens, "Oh that I had someone to hear me!" he says (31:35). The words of God, after those of Elihu, will show that God does hear him.

Both the silence that feels and the silence that listens are wise. But there are also silences that kill. Job feels himself obliged to break the silence and defend himself when it is suggested that he is in this inhuman situation through his own fault. He argues with his friends and with God. With facts from his own experience, Job affirms that an injustice has been committed. His discourse is one of life or death. If Job does not denounce the unjust order in which the innocent suffer, that order will be considered logical, and its irrationality will be declared rational. To keep silent is to die: "Who wants to contend with me? Because to be silent now would be to die" (3:19).[1] To his friends, he confesses that he is playing for all or nothing: "Keep silent for I am going to speak, and come whatever may come, I will risk it all" (13:13). This was his way of acting, even before falling into such misfortune (31:34). But his friends do not listen because they do not keep silent. God keeps silent, and this silence unleashes the outcries of Job.

The Cries

After the intense silence is shared for seven days and nights, it becomes unbearable, and the writing changes in rhythm and passion. The outcries of Job and his friends break the silence, and soon an uproar of arguments, concrete and abstract, takes over the garbage dump. There are thirteen speeches: six by Job, six by his friends (two each), and one by the young man Elihu. In the end, after all the words and arguments, the cries have still gone unanswered. God, inevitably, will also have to speak.

Job shouts out demanding justice, his voice filled with anger and anguish. Job curses the day he was born (3:1-3), demands to be heard, demonstrates his innocence, and contests, with arguments from daily life, the falseness of the doctrine of retribution. One can see, hear, and feel the tragedy.

When there is no response to his denunciations, Job assails God. The wise friends cannot permit such irreverence.[2] With well-known arguments, they try to drown out the cries of suffering. Outcry against outcry. One is trying to prove the innocence of the just, and others are searching for his guilt.

It seems that Job does not expect to be rewarded but wants merely to reclaim his dignity as a human. His most admirable quality is not that he does not curse God but rather that he never loses his dignity. Moreover, during his accusations and his defense, he grows in dignity: "Here is my signature, let the Almighty answer me, let my adversary write his allegations, I would carry it on my shoulder or fasten it on as a crown. He would be aware of my steps and I would approach him as a prince" (31:35-37). This is how Job finishes his last discourse. Hunger for God and hunger for humanity are inseparable.

The cries of Job are the cries that save. "To be silent now is to perish" (13:19). But the outcries of the others are useless. They are outside the concrete reference point that can serve to verify injustices. They defend the Almighty with statements that are out of sync with daily reality, condemning the just and themselves. Like Satan, the friends become the unintended accusers. Job claims: "I have heard a thousand speeches like this, all of you are bothersome consolers. Is there no limit to the empty words? . . . I could also talk as you do if I were in your place; I could string together words against you and shake my head against you, I could comfort you with my mouth and fill you moving my lips" (16:1-5).

At times, inopportune speeches can take such a hard line that they become like stones. Job feels this when he points out to his friends that their speeches are tormenting and crushing him (19:2). At this juncture some things become clear. Neither the silence nor the outcries are alleviating the suffering of the innocent. Job lives this situation in his own flesh. "Even though I speak, my pain is still with me, and yet when I am silent, my pain does not leave me" (16:6). At last God is forced to break the silence, come down to the garbage dump, and speak out. And since God is being questioned, God has the right to shout.

God rearranges the questions and expands the visions. God does not accuse Job, like Satan, the friends, or Elihu. God speaks of the cosmos. God situates human history within this wonderful cosmos. In a way, Job is right. God does not dodge the issue of disorder among humans. God recognizes that there are wrongdoers who are powerful and that there are those who suffer unjustly. But God does not simplify any answers or instruct Job on what has to be done. God introduces the complexity of human and cosmic existence so that Job may find all of the possible and unsuspected alternatives.

The dialogue between Job and God is mysteriously fruitful. The previous silence of God, in the face of the pain of the innocent, made it possible, with the wisdom of experience, to combat the theology that blames the innocent. And although Job was not aware of it, God was listening to his outcries. The roar of God (as revealed in the storm) and God's speaking open up Job's understanding. Job, in turn, keeps silence and listens to wisdom. The silences and calls from God are capable of moving one toward hope. During the most penetrating silences of God, when Job asks, "Where is my hope, who has seen it?" (17:15), he can then turn around and assure us in the next speech of the certainty that his avenger lives and that Job will see him face to face (19:25).

From the Commercial God to the God of Grace

In the book's epilogue Job is restored, but not because he did not curse God in spite of his adversities. To believe that would be capitulation to Satan and the wise men, affirming that God would trade or sell the restoration of Job in exchange for Job's not cursing.

Job does not curse God, but neither does he blessGod. Job complains of the injustice committed against the innocent and the just. God recognizes Job's demands; God does not accuse or blame Job. But neither does God say that Job is totally right. God is not the guilty one. God, like Job, simply recognizes the facts of the case. Both are aware of their limitations: God's limitations may be infinite mercy, even toward wrongdoers (since God has not dared to do away with them as yet, cf. 40:9-13); Job is limited by his smallness and his ignorance of God's grace: (40:4; 42:5). Both Job and God suffer from the lack of response to the cries of those who suffer from violence against them. So God proposes, through the complexity of the cosmos, to seek ways out of the dilemma.

In a utilitarian society such as ours it is crucial that we bring to light the grace of God. Today, when people do little for others, and merit is used as a condition of personhood, the God of grace reveals to us that all people, especially the Jobs, are persons of dignity by sheer grace—not by the number of their credit cards—and that persons are considered to be more valuable than mere things. As such, they are not to be discarded or auctioned off in the name of competion.

In our time, the bringing of grace into our lives is indispensable in order to confront the attractions of the god of commerce. This god tries to seduce us into successful careers so that we may be "number one" in everything and "be cool." This is a god who trades prestige in exchange for the purchase of brand-name products, who will exchange human dignity for power and money. It is a god who sells "humanity" in order to have the power of buying it back. But it is no longer human, it is plastic.

This god, invented by the marketplace, and, as such, an idol, has penetrated the religious world. Preachers present God as a kind of manager who heaps material goods on those who do his will. Businessmen, because of the uncertainty of their investments in a neoliberal market economy, worship this god. The poor, who are tired of their poverty, also place their bets on this god who can provide them with jobs, food, and color television. As yet, there is no awareness that the marketplace knows nothing of grace and mercy.

In the biblical text, Job is restored, but many others are not. The women and men who observe Job's fall and restoration were born into the world of misery and have always lived there. These folk, described in Job 30.1-10, are the ones whom the Salvadoran poet Roque Dalton[4] calls the "ones who are always suspicious of everything, the do-it-all, the sell-it-all, the eat-it-all, my compatriates, my brothers." The excluded ones are the Jobs of today and just their presence as a crucified body should terrify all of humanity. "Haggling over humanity," (an expression of Leopoldo Zea) is not something proper for humans, who are created in the image of God; but neither is insensitivity. Hunger for God is related to hunger for humanity—to be somebody, to exist with dignity.

In a free-market society, people do not count and only things have value. Or, in other words, the value of a person is measured in terms of how much that person can buy. It seems that in our day, the struggle for human rights (in the face of dictatorships) is becoming a struggle to be human (in the face of laws of the market place). In this race to achieve worldly success we become monsters, crushing our neighbors in order to save ourselves, enslaving ourselves in submitting to this logic.

Mission today implies, among other things, that we should try a thousand ways to recover the sensitivity among people and to reclaim solidarity with those who are excluded. To discern the right moments for silence and for crying out, the moments for listening and for embracing of the grace of God, is the first step.

Building a House for Everyone (1 Peter 2:1-10)

Most of us have at some time or other gone to a fair and visited the house of horrors. We buy a ticket and enter, eager for unexpected surprises. In the darkness, illogical things happen. A severed head suddenly appears. A human skeleton lays a hand on us from behind. We see flying objects. Someone tries to kill us with a machete or an ax. We scream in fright, clench our teeth, close our eyes, seize hold of a friend. The ax remains suspended in mid-air. In the end, we come out into the light, laughing, having known all along that the trip would end and that everything was make-believe.

I think that in our time we are often living in a house of horrors. Illogical and sometimes terrifying things happen. It rains when it shouldn't and vice versa; there is poison in the rivers; the stock market wildly shoots up and down; one boy assaults another to steal his tennis shoes; husbands beat and even kill their wives, and mothers beat and sometimes kill their children. Persons are considered disposable because they do not have the means to participate in the marketplace. Children, instead of going to school and sleeping safely in homes, live on the streets. Thousands of people who left their countries in order to work are sent back home against their will. In the same city block, one person dies of starvation while another spends money to lose weight. Our world house is a house of horrors. The difference between the one at the fair and our own is that in ours, we have paid the price since we were born: we can never leave the house, and, even worse, no one is surprised.

The mission that God has given to every one of us, from the North and South, the East and the West, is that together we become builders and living stones to remodel our world, to rebuild and redecorate a large house where there is room for everyone. Such a house will be illumined by the Spirit of God.

Constructing such a house leads us to think about the building stones. In 1 Peter, the author asks us to become living stones. What a strange concept: living stones. When we think of stones, we think of something without life, without movement. Yet, the author invites us to become living stones. How to comprehend such an invitation!

The letter, written near the end of the first century, was for migrants living in Pontus, Galatia, Cappadocia, and Bithynia. They were humble people going through very hard times: they were persecuted as Christians; they had no social status; they were poor; they were foreigners whose identities were always being questioned; they were full of fear and uncertainty. It reminds me of the situations that migrants face today in the United States, Europe, Costa Rica, Venezuela, and many other places throughout the world. The text insists on faith and hope. Surely that is what they needed in their severely hostile world. If we use the present situation as our context for the text of this epistle, perhaps we can understand what the author is saying. In 2:1-10, the text describes discarded stones, chosen stones, and living stones.

The Stone Discarded by the Builder

The great challenge we face today as Christians is the infinite number of people who are not taken seriously as persons. The woman who is beaten and raped is not considered a person by the rapist. The unemployed are not considered persons by the system that currently causes the unemployment. The indigenous are not considered persons when their lands are taken away. Blacks are not considered persons when they are pushed aside because of the color of their skin. Retirees are not considered persons when their pensions are cut. Children are not considered persons when the economic system forces them to live and work in the streets. Our society, based on the market economy with its neoliberal policies, produces nonpersons. The challenge we face in our own mission is to confront such dehumanization.

Many stones have been discarded by the builders of today's society. They are the excluded, the leftovers of the system. That human beings are considered disposable is intolerable. They are the discarded stones from the construction of the house, our world, our planet, where there should be room for all.

In Peter's epistle, we find that to reinforce the hope and faith of his readers the author invites them to come close and to firmly hold on to the strong and living stone, Jesus the Messiah, who was also excluded by the Roman and Jewish societies. Because of sin that builds mansions for the few, and because of God's love and solidarity with humanity, Jesus Christ also became a stone rejected by the builders, as quoted in 2:7, referring to Psalm 118:22.

In order to be part of a building that is good for everyone, it is vital that the living stones be chosen for their excellence. In his letter, Peter exhorts his readers to flee all malice, hypocrisy, falseness, deceit, and envy (2:1). We need wisdom to decide which path to take at the crossroads that confront us every day. And we are not always right. Our society is tricky. If, as missionaries, we are living stones, how can we give life to the dead stones?

The epistle exhorts its readers to taste the good milk, unadulterated, from our mother God, so that we can grow up in health and save ourselves from this perverse world. We need to experience, like infants, the taste of God, to experience God's grace and love in the midst of misfortune and the daily demands that cheapen our humanity (2:2). Deceit and envy are poisoned foods, but the maternal milk from God is good and nurturing food: we should never go against the humanity of the human species.

The Discarded Stone Is Chosen

The fact that the stones are being cast aside is a scandal. Paul spoke of the scandal of the cross. Jesus, in the way he lived, in his manner of being, in his passion, death, and resurrection, was a scandal in one way or another, in one group or another. In our day it seems that the cross has ceased to be a scandal, and no one sees anything irrational about the scandal of the excluded. If it is a scandal that Jesus was a stone rejected by the builders, then, for many, it is even more scandalous that the rejected stone is considered precious and is chosen by God: "Come close to him, the living stone, discarded by the human beings, but chosen by God and precious" (2:4). And with Jesus, the discarded stones cast out in the ravines are the favored ones of God. The society excludes those who are not able to compete, those who do not have value, money, power, light skin color. But God, in his solidarity of love, his mercy and faithfulness, raises them up with his grace to a "chosen lineage" (2:9).

Today, the theme of grace is central in a society that increasingly closes off spaces for grace and imposes its own laws of worth as conditions of success. The ways of God are strange to our society. The unwanted are called the beloved of God. In 2:10 we are told, "Once you were not a people, but now you are God's people; once you had not received mercy, but now you have received mercy."

Jesus Christ, the discarded stone, is chosen by God to form the foundation of a new social architecture in which the rights and the dignity of all persons are respected. The main cornerstone (2:6), the head of the angle (2:7), this living stone is placed at the very foundation and base of the house. From below, it guarantees that all the other stones in this building are alive and solid. Thus the house will have its own identity, have room for everyone, and be very beautiful. Our mission, which is also God's mission, is to build this house, with Christ, the stone discarded by the builders, as the guarantee that the house will fit everyone. For those of us who think it is possible to build such a house, the text in 2:6 tells us that we will not be put to shame, that we will not fail.

The builders who rejected the stone do not believe. Those responsible for the structure of our society, this house of horrors, do not believe in either grace or mercy. They believe only in the dehumanizing production of great surplus, without considering the inequalities and exclusions created by the process. Therefore, they deny whatever utopia will separate them from their interests. According to Peter, the corner stone for the new house becomes a stumbling block, a rock on the abyss that will make the unbelievers fall. I believe it is time to recover the image of Jesus Christ as the stumbling block or rock of the abyss. But this is possible only if we contrast the cornerstone of the house we want to build with the house of horrors in which we barely exist today.

We Are Called

God calls us to be living stones and to build a house with room for us all. Peter tells us, "Like living stones, let yourselves be built into a spiritual house, to be a holy priesthood, to offer spiritual sacrifices acceptable to God through Jesus Christ (2:5) is theological because it uses cultural terminology. And that is precisely what we need. In order to conceive of all the earth as a temple, Paul tells us in 1 Corinthians 6:29 that our bodies are temples of the Holy Spirit. To do a modern paraphrase of the text we could say that an extremely important part of our mission is to be builders of a house in which the Spirit can dwell. If we are living stones, the Spirit will fill all and illumine all. We are called to build a house in which all persons will feel important and loved. This implies constructing a society in which civic groups encourage decentralized operations and where self-management is sustained—that there be true democracy at all levels. "Real priesthood" for all affirms such democracy.

To be of a chosen lineage is another strong affirmation subject to misunderstanding. If this declaration was made for the marginalized immigrants of Asia Minor, it cannot be interpreted as a call urging them to feel superior to others. It is important that those in the original audience recognize their dignity and their worth and have a sense of belonging. Therefore, God calls us to be living stones and to build a new house where we can live happily with respect for all cultures. What sort of house, then, do we want?

We want a house with a large kitchen, an enormous dining room, and enough food for everyone. There needs to be a large living room where we can gather with friends. It should have a huge garden, with many hammocks, where the children, youth, adults, and the elderly can swing and play without fear and can enjoy the beauty of nature, its plants and animals, the rivers and hillsides, the stars and entire universe, a place where nature is regarded as friend, is not threatened, but is cared for by all. The house also needs sufficient bedrooms and decent bathrooms for persons of each culture to affirm their own identity and to enjoy their bodies—as women, as men, as black, white, brown, or yellow. The house should have a tremendous workshop, where everyone can have a job and never be fired or forced to retire. And there must be be all kinds of musical instruments for the celebrations and festivals. In a house like that, the Spirit of God will dwell.

The term "living stones" connotes strength, stability, and, at the same time, dynamism and heart. Today we need all these qualities in order to build the house of our dreams. And we have a right to dream. We ask God to accompany us with his wisdom to create, for everyone, models of mission in the construction of his house, our home.

And the World Became Flesh (Galatians)

Some time ago, Jung Mo Sung gave me an advertisement for Nike tennis shoes that had appeared in the newspaper *Folha de São Paulo* on March 2, 1994. Among other things, it said the following:

> Nike is sublime. [It has] mature construction and is violently sophisticated within what is available in the world of marketing. A relationship of affection [exists] between a product and its consumer. Nike is not a tennis shoe; it is a life style. Nike is a model and a vision of the world. [Nike's] ads are like gospel. Not only do they sell, they indoctrinate. They don't only convince, they convert. . . . It is this world of Nike that a sedentary person like myself is getting when purchasing the tennis shoe. Nike makes the young man in the American suburbs, or the kid in the Midwest or Sutton Place feel as though he is a basketball player from Harlem, and that is "cool, man." Nike makes a divorced woman with cellulite feel like Fernanda Keller, just because she did three laps around the ball court wearing Nikes. Of course Nike makes the "boy" in the third world feel [as] good as if he were sniffing glue. . . . If [a young boy] didn't [have Nikes] he would die. The boy is head and toes Nike.

In Colombia, a frequent advertisement in the newspapers and on television states that neither Christ nor the saints can do miracles today, but that a certain well-known bank can. There seems to be open competition between the mission of the free market and the mission of Christ. The market also has its theology. We might call it "the other gospel," like the one criticized by Paul in his letter to the Galatians.

Today we are witnessing a confrontation of two "gospels": one that leads to life and freedom; another that, even though it speaks of freedom, leads to servitude. The reality of exclusion, dehumanization, fragmentation, callousness, and the scarcity of alternatives cries out for the manifestation of God in our house—the house where all humans dwell. Like Job, we want God to be present—not to say who is right, or to explain the causes of injustice, but to become "in the flesh" the Emmanuel and to participate with us all in the anguish, the silences and outcries, the desires, and, yes, the fiestas. Our theme speaks of the good news of the gospel: "And the word became flesh."

Christ frees us from the perverse world and the law. In his greeting to the Galatians, Paul includes a Christological formula that is the oldest of the primitive tradition. Speaking of Jesus Christ, he writes: "[He] gave himself for our sins to set us free from the present evil age, according to the will of our God and Father" (1:4). Here, in a few words, we have the liberation from the present evil age, the desire of God to free his creatures, and the saving mediation of Christ.

The fundamental fact is that we, as human beings, are liberated by Christ from the present evil age. Many have understood the text in an individualistic, intimate, and dualistic manner. God takes me out of the world because it is evil. Such a statement leads to irrelevant theology and a rejection of political involvement. What we have to rethink is the meaning of liberation and its relationship to the present evil age (or perverse world) from which Christ is saving us. We talk of liberation when experiencing oppression. Paul contrasts two powers: Christ and the world. This world, however, is not the creation of God; it is the perverse world of oppression and enslavement. That is why we speak of liberation. The affirmation that Christ saves us from the perverse world is fundamental and universal—valid for the Galatians and for us today. The relevance of the message is in our discernment of the age in which we live and in identifying the current perversity. The message of Christ is good news only when it is relevant and when it generates change in our attitude and behavior toward the cosmos, our neighbor, and God.

In 1:4, Paul uses the Greek word *ekseletai*, which means "to liberate." Here he is not using the common terms the Greeks use for salvation, but the images of a slave and a free person. He could have used the word *apolutro*, which is "to rescue," "to redeem," as used in other Christological forms (Romans 3:24). *Apolutro* was the term used secularly to buy the freedom of slaves. Thanks to the *peculium*, the payment of ransom, a slave could change status and become free. The use of *ekseletai* strictly contrasts the status of the slave and that of the free. Here in Galatians, Paul speaks of liberation without a trace of the stigma of slavery. In fact, the term is an echo of the Israelites' liberation from Egypt. The liberation Paul refers to here is very radical. It refers to a human emancipation that goes far beyond the social and the political. It is the growing consciousness of an individual's right to be human, to be free of any slavery and structure that diminishes human dignity and self control. It does not exclude the political or the economic, but it centers on the fundamental awareness of being a free person in a community of freedom, and of living and being part of a beautiful cosmos that should be cared for. It covers everything, including racism, sexism, despotism, even oneself. The only thing excluded from this liberation is the freedom to enslave, kill, diminish the dignity of others, or destroy nature.

As Christians, we reject very quickly the gift of being free subjects, owners of our own destiny. We have a deep concern about human frailty and the power of sin that leads us away from God. That is why we quickly emphasize that although we are free from sin we are still slaves to Christ. It is a legitimate concern. As humans we are frail and often do not know how to use our freedom. Nevertheless, if Christ frees us from the evil world in order to make us his slaves, we cannot talk about the grace of God. Before we can do so, we need to affirm the act of full liberation mentioned in Galatians. To be free from the present evil world is to discern its evil, to take our distance from it, to be critical, and, of course, not to let ourselves be caught up in the flow of its injustice, racism, patriarchalism, exclusion, and antihuman regulations. To be free is to feel oneself in communion with God, other humans, and the entire universe.

The most ancient explanation for this liberation is that Christ gave himself for our sins. Another formula states that Christ was "handed over" (Romans 4:25) or that "God gave him" (8:32). The formulation "Christ gave himself for our sins" suggests self-atonement. There is in this statement a clear influence from Judaism, and according to Jewish thought, the righteous who suffer martyrdom can atone for the sins of others.

We can ask ourselves why liberation from the evil world occurs when Christ hands himself over for our sins. The question is a hard one. We have become accustomed to a blind repetition of dogma, without reflecting on its meaning for today. I believe that in the act of giving himself, Christ makes liberation possible because the act of giving introduces another kind of logic into the world of evil. It is the logic of grace. In a society of "save your self if you can," nobody is saved; there is no grace, no solidarity, no awareness of personal freedom. Whoever tries to save only his own life will lose it.

Dominated by the logic of looking for our own salvation in the world of competition, we enter into a world of sin and will constantly sin against anyone and everyone in our way. In a society of "save yourself if you can," we all become sinners, even against our will. To put an end to this mortal logic, Jesus Christ, the human face of God, dramatically calls attention to a new logic, unknown in today's depraved world. It is the logic of grace, the logic of infinite love. It is a logic that no longer measures sacrifices because Jesus Christ has taken that on once and for all. We are not going to ask for anyone's sacrifice or call for sacrificing the sacrificers. The atoning sacrifice has been concluded on the cross of Golgotha. The crucified body of Jesus demonstrates not only the solidarity that God has for his creatures but also what a society is capable of doing. The resurrection of this body shows what God wants for those who are crucified. In Galatians 1:1, Paul begins his greetings with the event of the resurrection of Jesus Christ. God wants the liberation of all creatures and their habitat, the creation, and the resurrection of the one whom society assassinated because he gave himself for the sins of everyone.

Paul deliberately includes this Christology in his letter to the Galatians because he sees danger in the preaching of those who favored Jewish law, and fears that they have forgotten the freedom they had embraced. Following the law could be a threat to the freedom that they already enjoy in Christ. In chapter 4, Paul again presents the Christology in new terms:

> But when the fullness of time had come, God sent his Son, born of a woman, born under the law, in order to redeem those who were under the law, so that we might receive adoption as children. And because you are children, God has sent the Spirit of his Son into our hearts, crying, "Abba!" Father! So you are no longer a slave but a child, and if a child then also an heir, through God." (4:7)

In our society of "save yourself if you can" reigns the logic of the law. We all try to save ourselves by following the dictates of the law imposed by the neoliberal market society. We think that if we don't play by the rules of the marketplace we are lost. Yet, if we do comply faithfully with these laws, without any kind of interference, many people will be left out. To hear that one can be free from the law, from the sense of an external and enslaving logic, would, indeed, be good news—not only in the days of Paul but also in our own modern world, a world in which we function at such an accelerated, demanding, and self-destructive tempo.

The gospel announces that you are free and a person of dignity not because you fulfill the law but because of God's grace and mercy toward his creatures. Whoever submits to the law becomes a slave. When I speak of the law, I refer to any law, institution, or tradition that tends to enslave you. You do not need the values of commercial society to be considered a person. What you need is to accept that in Christ, God became human, a free person, in order to show us the logic of faith as seen in his own life.

In Galatians 4:6, Paul uses the image of sons and daughters of God. To be called a son or daughter of God is to be considered a person of dignity. The Roman emperors called themselves sons of God and thought themselves divine. The Jews also considered themselves to be sons and daughters of God because of the alliance God made with the Israelites. But Paul makes it very clear that the divine affiliation occurs through faith and not through compliance with the law or because of privileged lineage, gender, ethnic group, or color. In the Christological event, we observe once again God's complete solidarity with all humanity, cultural and material: "Born of woman and under the law" unmasks the logic of this depraved world, and it is faith in his life of faith that does it. Liberation comes from below and consists of abolishing enslavement to laws and of turning slaves into free sons and daughters of God. Those who are free from the law can have their own words, their own voice. Before, the law would take possession of them and impose its path on them. Now they are persons who can claim Abba, Father (Mother), and become free sons and daughters.

The message is directed to all of us. The discussion between Paul and his opponents was precisely whether among the people of God there would be room for non-Jews who had not been circumcised.

By declaring liberation from the law, the message becomes universal. It reaches all who want to walk in accordance with the logic of faith or the Spirit, no matter what their nation or culture. This logic, says Paul in Romans, is the one that embraces life, justice, and peace. That is why we need to insist that liberty go beyond liberation from alienating laws. Because, in order to live together in freedom, human beings need a guide who consistently challenges them to renewal of their consciousness and their behavior. That is the Spirit. That is why Paul says clearly that, in the end, what really matters is the "faith that works out of love" or the "new creation."

This statement does not mean that since God is good to all, all peoples should love the Christian God. In the act of incarnation of the Word, value is given to creation in all its diversity. In the incarnation, many cultures are affirmed with all of their ambiguities. The fact that Jesus was a Jew and a male does not mean that we should all follow Jewish culture and imitate Jewish men. Jesus was born of a woman in history because God values history, and God's desire is that this history and habitat be recreated. Yet, we are not to adopt the prevailing culture uncritically. In all cultures there are signs of life and death, of enslavement and freedom. Paul himself rejects the imposition of circumcision—the identity of Jewish culture—onto other cultures. And yet, he also criticizes those elements of the Galatians' culture—"the elements of the world" (4:8-10), that were enslaving them, determining their existence, and causing them to live in fear.

When they say "Abba," the persons or nations who say it become brothers and sisters because they are bound together as the sons and daughters of the same Father-Mother. It has been said that this affiliation is the historical foundation for solidarity. It is also possible for us as Christians to strengthen our ties with other cultures that communicate with God by using their own words for God, such as Father-Mother, Pachamama, Paba and Nana.

In the end, Christian freedom, according to Paul's letter to the Galatians, is a total opposite to the freedom being offered by modern societies. Evangelizing in present-day societies is offering an invitation to become human, to be free with dignity and a sense of belonging. At the same time, we must challenge and deny the authority of "the other gospel" that is being proclaimed by a neoliberal market society. Let us, then, hold on to the words of Paul: "For freedom Christ has set us free. Stand firm, therefore, and do not submit again to a yoke of slavery"(5:1).

End Notes

1. In this and other biblical quotations I am following the translation of A. Schoekel, *The Pilgrim Bible*, Bilbao, 1993.
2. The text is full of legal terminology. Job is trying to establish a lawsuit against God. The friends are lawyers defending God (Job 13:8). Cf. A. Schoekel and J. L. Siere, *Job*, Madrid, 1983.
3. G. Gutierrez, ibid, p. 173.
4. R. Dalton, *Las historias prohibidas del pulgarcito*, El Salvador, 1992.

The São Paulo Process:
An Experience of Sharing Beyond
Material Resources

The São Paulo Process was begun in May 1986, when representatives of sixty-four programs and projects in Latin America and the Caribbean met with representatives of the National Council of the Churches of Christ in the USA for the purpose of mutual evaluation.

Evaluation by U.S. church agencies and mission boards of the projects and programs they were funding was nothing unusual. However, evaluation of those boards and agencies by representatives of the programs and projects being funded was a radical departure. The conference was so successful that it was agreed to start an ongoing process of sharing, of discovering one another, and of growing together. At its most fundamental, the São Paul Process was, and continues to be, an attempt to put into practice what the gospel demands. We who are engaged in that process want to find new ways of sharing material resources—within both donor and recipient churches—and of sharing the Body of Christ.

One year later, in Atlanta, participants reaffirmed the process. Very few persons from the United States had gone to the São Paulo meeting. Afterwards, when questioned, they confessed that they had been afraid of inadvertently controlling the meeting. However, when the Latin Americans stated that they wanted to talk as equals, another meeting was arranged, where representatives of the mission agencies and of participants from Latin America discussed the proposal.

And so it was that in 1989 in Indianapolis, participants evaluated the first three years of the fledgling São Paulo Process: what was accomplished; what was not; what were its weakness; what were its strengths. To their joy, they realized that they had discovered a new model for working together in creative and collegial ways which, until then, had seemed impossible. Let it be said that there were many who openly questioned the hidden agenda of the mission boards: "Why are they opening their doors? Why are they opening their books? Why are they talking with us in a serious way? Why are they letting us participate?" There was much suspicion, well expressed by the Spanish saying, "When the alms are too large, even the saints get suspicious." However, with all of its flaws, the São Paulo Process was off and running.

Ultimately, the process will result in abandoning practices that have endured for one hundred fifty years in Latin America and the Caribbean. Our goal is not only to discover new relationships between North and South, but between South and South as well. At a 1992 evaluation, there was general agreement that the São Paulo Process has helped break through the isolation and prejudice that existed between groups in different countries by providing the opportunity for sharing experiences and concerns, and by getting to know one another personally.

Those who have been the traditional objects of diaconal and missionary concern need to have the space to express themselves: to communicate their needs, culture, and expectations. The São Paulo Process does not operate in one direction only, that is, from North to South, or top to bottom. Rather, persons engaged in diaconal ministry and mission according to the São Paulo Process are engaged in a mutual search to discover God's purpose. In this process, the teacher learns by teaching and the students teach by learning.

The Costa Rica consultation tried to maintain this richness. For the first time, theological and missiological debate was not the exclusive patrimony of theologians and clerics. The consultation included among its participants working women, peasants, indigenous peoples, people of African descent, community leaders, grassroots communities, and youth, all symbols of a society that has excluded them—the ones whom Jesus Christ called to be the first citizens in God's reign. They participated in debates; they were engaged in making decisions; they revealed to their fellow participants how the power and the love of God is manifested in the lives of the poor and excluded. In this and other ways, the Missiology Conference in Costa Rica exemplified what it is that the São Paulo Process is trying to build into mission for a new millennium.

Statements by Denominational Delegates from the United States Prepared at the Missiology Consultation, San José, Costa Rica, April 21-25, 1997

■

African Methodist Episcopal Church
African Methodist Episcopal Zion Church

Although we have not yet held a formal meeting about these crucial issues, we were pleased to be involved in the consultation, look forward to receiving the final report, and will seek ways of incorporating these findings into our models of mission.

■

American Baptist Churches

It is important to reexamine traditional emphases on training and education so that members of congregations will become increasingly aware of the diversity of the Christian family.

Exchanges of personnel, history, and experience are important—within as well as among the confessions—in order to open new horizons and to strengthen ecumenical ties. Special but not exclusive emphasis should be placed on South-South exchanges.

It is important to take advantage of the ecumenical opportunities for encounter and cooperation presented by the historical circumstances that challenge our people, for example, church-state relations in Mexico, the relationship between Puerto Rico and the United States, and so forth.

There is great concern about the widening distance—if not chasm—between the awareness of consciousness of leaders, who participate in meetings and conferences such as this one, and that of the grass roots. This distance makes it more difficult to put the pretty speeches into ecclesial practice.

As Baptists, part of the radical Anabaptist reform, we are heirs to a rich tradition of being in the minority. From that perspective, we recognize and celebrate the diversity of criteria, which is basic to an inclusive Christian witness. We say this recognizing our great need also to learn from other confessions.

We recognize the need to escape from our denominational limitations even while we question what we have heard at this consultation, namely, that the Pentecostal model will be the future for churches in Latin America.

■

Church of the Brethren

Since March 1995, the Church of the Brethren has been going through a period of reorganization and downsizing. Personnel as well as portfolios have been reduced, and our mission focus has been narrowed. Two guiding documents, a board mission statement and a core function statement, have guided us to refocus our energy toward congregational life. The intent is to revitalize and reconnect our congregations with our mission beyond our own membership. A new body is being formed to discern and process new mission initiatives emerging from congregations before they become action.

This redesign has been developed and driven by our elected general board. This missiology consultation is timely as we continue to plan for the future. We will attempt to act on the considerations suggested below, always in light of the financial realities faced by the Church of the Brethren in its reorganization process.

Suggested initiatives upon returning home:

1. To develop or expand the educational opportunities for sister-to-sister congregations and other new initiatives such as work camps, educational visits, and tours, Brethren volunteer orientation, training programs, seminary education, and retraining of board staff. The purpose and the initiatives of this consultation need to be included in such an educational process.

2. To examine our mission philosophy in light of the issues and challenges presented in this consultation.

3. To develop guidelines for mission planning that include ideas and responses from those to be served. "Common space" is needed to avoid the errors of the past.

4. To make use of the Brethren witness for peace, justice, and the core of the earth by informing congregations and shaping their witness in public and foreign policy.

5. To retain and develop ecumenical partnerships and alliances whenever possible in the planning or implementing of new iniatives.

6. To include persons representing a variety of languages and ethnic groups in congregational life, as staff, and, if possible, in our central office.

◼

The Episcopal Church

1. As Anglicans we should refresh our history, reaffirm our commitments and be aware of resources that serve as the foundation for ecumenical relations, making these known within the Anglican Communion.

2. Anglican pastoral ministry and ethos should be deepened since they bring us closer to the ecumenical world, as demonstrated not only at the global level—our participation in the creation of the World Council of Churches' Faith and Order Movement—but also at the national level.

3. Anglican historical commitment and identity should give credibility to our genuine ecumenical participation.

4. Anglican liturgical spaces should be shared with others because common participation in liturgy prepares us for common action, such as Anglican participation in training programs in South India and the current dialogue between Anglicans and Lutherans.

5. Development of inter-Anglican relations should be promoted since the Anglican Communion is a fellowship of regional autonomous churches in which such open relationships makes us reciprocally vulnerable. This should also be valuable training for further ecumenical relationships.

6. Inter-Anglican exchanges should be promoted in several directions, especially South-South and South-North. There have not been enough of these and every exercise is training for ecumenical exchange.

7. The new missionary vision within the Anglican communion is being challenged by Pentecostal forms of worship (vis-à-vis Anglican liturgy). In an ecumenical relationship this challenge does not mean that by continuing to observe liturgical forms we discard the gifts of the Spirit, which are expressed in a deep commitment of faith.

8. To share ecumenically any information about a possible Jubilee. The churches have the right to ask for pardon of the external debt in view of their generous contributions to Third World development—far more than the World Bank and the International Monetary Fund, and interest-free.

9. The Jubilee should lead us to a conversion (a changing of) the system in which it will become transformed from ruler to partner— a partner who can receive the forgiveness of the poor and strive for reconciliation.

10. Jubilee 2000 will be a macro-ecumenical offering to humanity. A biblical interpretation of the Jubilee is needed in order to prepare us for that which will happen after the debt has been pardoned.

- South-South leadership needs to be promoted. This has been done among certain countries, but needs greater emphasis and direction.
- South-South missionaries can change the prevailing image of "comfortable" missionaries.
- We can take better advantage of opportunities for ecumenical theological education, taking advantage of already existing institutions.
- Efforts in social action and shared pastoral ministry—especially in cases of emergency, disaster, AIDS ministry, prison ministry, and so forth—can all help to develop closer relationships among the communions. A concrete case of shared ministry in the Caribbean could be agricultural development.

■

Evangelical Lutheran Church in America

In our denomination we have inherited an ecumenical vocation that has its roots in the Augsburg Confession. Therefore, we cannot speak about initiating but rather, accelerating a process already begun. As a denomination, we are members of all the councils represented here. Our presence is a reflection of our ecumenical vocation.

We realize that we continue to confront our limitations. It is important and a demand of our times to overcome anything that is an obstacle to cooperation and ecumenical challenge. We mention the following limitations:

1. Although we proclaim ourselves to be ecumenical, our ecumenism does not reach the bases of our denomination. Ecumenism remains limited to the leaders. In the last thirty years, there has been an attempt to call for an opening to ecumenical relations and social problems. This process has often been slow.

2. We believe that we should strive for a common and more testimonial witness. Some experiences point in this direction, as in

Chile, Bolivia, Central America, and Brazil, where political and social struggle has often been accompanied by a diaconal, prophetic, and celebratory ecumenism.

3. As a result of theological practice and reflection, we feel that we must continue to work toward an understanding of ecumenism in our congregations. Our practice of ecumenism comes from the theology of the cross and is our theological contribution.

■

Presbyterian Church (USA)

1. Seminarians should spend some time in an ecumenical seminary.

2. Learn to understand our own confessional tradition in order to function in the ecumenical arena with greater integrity.

3. Hold meetings at the base level.

4. Develop partnerships between confessional and ecumenical bodies.

5. Ask each local church to invite a local church from another confession to share time and space with one another.

6. Issue reports about what happened at this conference; share testimonies.

7. Receive analyses of situations; stop accusations; work toward reconciliation.

8. Remember that the cross is present in all confessions; act as members of the larger family.

9. Continue the process of education patiently and persistently, using the *Book of Order* as a guide and source of inspiration. Remember that education begins at all levels. Put the cross into education.

10. Participate in ecumenical efforts within the Presbyterian family, getting to know one another as Presbyterians in the United States, Guatemala, and Cuba.

■

Reformed Church in America

The Reformed Church in America works ecumenically. For example, in Honduras we work with the Moravian Church. Norvelle Goff-Rudy is the only mission worker present at this consultation. The RCA will continue to work ecumenically since there are no churches of our denomination outside the United States and Canada.

The RCA is refocusing attention on the poor in cities throughout the world. It is our dream to set up worldwide missiological training centers.

■

Common Ministry: United Church of Christ-Christian Church (Disciples of Christ)

The UCC and Disciples want to carry out a global ministry. There is still work that needs to be done ecumenically so that our churches may learn to know and understand one another.

If steps are being taken in the United States toward full communion with churches in certain Latin American countries, we need to make a substantial effort to help the churches feel called to a common mission.

In this process, relationships of the denominational tradition have a great deal of influence, for example, relationships with councils of churches such as CONASPEH (Spiritual Council of Churches in Haiti), where there is no marked denominational history and where a global ministry is accepted as completely normal. Still, although it is an ecumenical institution, some difficulty remains in using the term "ecumenical."

It is important to assume responsibility for ministry toward the excluded and toward dealing with such difficult issues as homosexuality, abortion, and AIDS.

Attention to Latin American migrants should be a topic of discussion for churches in the United States and Latin America.

■

United Methodist Church

First, we realized that there is still a long road to travel before we can answer these questions with integrity. Why? Because there are many issues within the confessional family itself that we need to work on together with greater harmony. So far, we have not been able to achieve this. In other words, as we attempt to answer these questions we confess that there is much we must learn and that we must recognize the seriousness of internal conflicts within the United Methodist Church.

We celebrate the times when we have worked together with other denominations, and recognize the value that the Pentecost paradigm provides for unity in diversity—in which distinctive characteristics are conserved without causing divisions within the body of Christ.

We must work together on many issues—issues that cross borders and denominational lines such as unmasking false gods of the market, and struggles for justice and against impunity.

We recognize that often ecumenical work emerges in moments of crisis, especially around natural and artificial disasters and issues of justice. Examples of such issues and places are the struggle in Nicaragua, Panama after the U.S. invasion, Guatemala, and many others.

It is important to develop an understanding of what constitutes a crisis. The crisis in Nicaragua has not ended, but interest has declined greatly. Today, CNN and other mass media are defining for us what and where a crisis is. Does the strength of ecumenical work depend on the dictates of CNN?

External and internal elements needed in order to attain an ecumenical will:

External

We need to increase the level of confidence in ecumenical mechanisms or institutions. We are concerned about the way in which the National Council of the Churches of Christ in the USA is not distancing itself critically from the present U.S. administration. There should also be a recognition that internal administrative policy decisions affect levels of confidence.

Internal

1. Education for our members. A serious effort needs to be mounted from the pulpit to speak about the importance of our relationships with different partners in mission.
2. Mission education should promote ecumenical sharing of different resources in many directions.
3. Sharing through a wide range of information materials about cases where giving a common witness has helped to preserve or improve life.
4. The importance of abstaining from arrogance.
5. We must commit ourselves to
   - not undermining the ministry of partners in mission;
   - not imposing our points of view or interfering in the internal matters of other churches;
   - being ready to engage in dialogue and offer critical solidarity.

We recognize that churches today are experiencing many crises. In this context it will be a mistake to limit ourselves to finding ways for mission agencies to work together more effectively. We understand that there is a need for ecclesiological debate of greater depth. We must also speak about ways of renewing the churches.

We need to continue these conversations. Follow-up should include consideration of what issues need to be studied in greater depth.

We need to enter into direct dialogue with leaders of the Pentecostal churches. In view of the high visibility given to Pentecostalism in this consultation, we think it unfortunate that we did not hear directly from Pentecostals. The topic needs to be treated more seriously.

Conference Participants

DENOMINATIONAL DELEGATES FROM THE UNITED STATES

African Methodist Episcopal Church

McKinley Young, Chair, Commission on Missions, Atlanta, Georgia

Dorothy R. Young, Member, Church World Service & Witness Committee, Atlanta, Georgia

Dorothy A. Peck, President, Washington, D.C.

Robert V. Webster, Presiding Bishop, Sixteenth District, Jacksonville, Florida

Cherie F. Bellamy, Executive Director, Service and Development Agency, Inc., Washington, D.C.

African Methodist Episcopal Zion Church

Kermit J. DeGraffenreidt, Secretary-Treasurer, Department of Overseas Missions, New York, New York

American Baptist Churches

Stan Slade, Associate Director, Overseas Division, Valley Forge, Pennsylvania

Lillian Solt, Overseas Division, Valley Forge, Pennsylvania

Ruth Orantes, Latin American Baptist Seminary, Santa Ana, El Salvador

Adalia Gutiérrez, Managua, Nicaragua

Sara Wiegner, Baptist Convention of Costa Rica

Johnny Saborio, Baptist Church "Fuente de Luz," Costa Rica

Lázaro González, Baptist Seminary of Mexico

Church of the Brethren

Mervin Keeney, Director, Global Mission Partnership, Elgin, Illinois

Mariana Barriga, Coordinator, Latin America and the Caribbean Office, Elgin, Illinois

Glen Timmons, Executive, Parish Ministries Commission, Elgin, Illinois

Guillermo Encarnación, Hispanic Ministries, Elgin, Illinois

Episcopal Church

Ricardo Potter-Norman, Associate Director, Anglican and Global Relations, New York, New York

Thomas Prichard, Executive Director, South America Missionary Society, SAMS, Ambridge, Pennsylvania

Dorothy Gist, Mission Personnel Officer, New York, New York

Edmundo Desueza-Fleury, Executive Secretary, Caribbean Region, Santo Domingo, Dominican Republic

Titus Presler, Rector, St. Peter's Episcopal Church, Cambridge, Massachusetts

Evangelical Lutheran Church in America

Bonnie L. Jensen, Executive Director, Division of Global Mission, Chicago, Illinois

Rafael Malpica-Padilla, Program Director, South and Central America, Chicago, Illinois

Will L. Herzfeld, Director for Global Mission, Chicago, Illinois

Walter Baires, Iglesia Luterana "La Resurrección," San Salvador, El Salvador

Diana M. Valdez, Spokane, Washington

Martin Junge, Evangelical Lutheran Church in Chile

Rui Bernhard, Mission Secretary, Porto Alegre, Brazil

James Lochan, Head Office, Lutheran Church in Guyana

Lorenzo Uturunco Mamani, Bolivian Evangelical Lutheran Church

Loretta Horton, Director, Social Ministries for Congregations, Chicago, Illinois

Presbyterian Church (USA)

Syngman Rhee, Associate Director, Ecumenical Partnership Program, Louisville, Kentucky

Eriberto Soto, Associate for South America and Mexico, Louisville, Kentucky

Patty Lane, Associate for Program Development, Self Development of People Program, Louisville, Kentucky

Julia Ann Moffett, Associate, Central America and the Caribbean, Louisville, Kentucky

Eugene McKelvey, Houston, Texas

Gerson Mendonça de Annunçiacão, Secretary of the Church Mission, Independent Presbyterian Church of Brazil

Enock Coelho de Assis, Executive Secretary, Missions Secretariat, Independent Presbyterian Church of Brazil

Gadiel Gomez, National Evangelical Presbyterian Church, Guatemala City, Guatemala

Edelberto Valdéz Fleites, Reformed Presbyterian Church, Havana, Cuba

Reformed Church in America

Roger De Young, Liaison for Mexico and Venezuela, Grand Rapids, Michigan

Norvelle Goff-Rudy, Evangelical Moravian Clinic, Honduras

United Church of Christ-Christian Church (Disciples of Christ)

Daniel F. Romero, General Secretary, United Church Board World
Ministries, New York, New York

David A. Vargas, Executive, Latin America and the Caribbean, Common
Global Ministries Board, Indianapolis, Indiana

Raquel Rodriguez, Program Assistant, Common Global Ministries Board,
Indianapolis, Indiana

Manuel de la Rosa, Chair, Latin America and the Caribbean, Common
Global Ministries Board, El Paso, Texas

Patrick Villier, CONASPEH, Port-au-Prince, Haiti

United Methodist Church

Peggy Hutchison, Associate General Secretary, Global Network and
Ecumenical Relations, New York, New York

Michael G. Rivas, Deputy General Secretary, Planning and Research,
General Board of Global Ministries, New York, New York

German Acevedo, Assistant General Secretary, Community Ministries,
General Board of Global Ministries, New York, New York

Mario Nicolas, Vice Pres., CIEMAL, Colón, Panama

Bishop Aldo Etchegoyen, Council of Bishops in Latin America, Buenos
Aires, Argentina

DENOMINATIONAL DELEGATES FROM CANADA

Chris Ferguson, Area Secretary, Caribbean and Latin America, Division of
World Outreach, The United Church of Canada, Etobicoke, Ontario,
Canada

COUNCILS

Caribbean Conference of Churches

Gerard Granado, Associate General Secretary, Glencoe, Trinidad

Latin American Council of Churches

Walter Altmann, President, São Leopoldo, Brazil

Felipe Adolf, General Secretary, Quito, Ecuador

World Council of Churches

Anna Langerak, Director of Unit II, Geneva, Switzerland

Brenda Ruiz, Evangelical Association of Family Counseling—AEDAF,
Managua, Nicaragua

Israel Batista, Geneva, Switzerland

Roman Catholic Church

Thomas Henehan, M.M., Maryknoll Fathers and Brothers (Catholic Foreign Mission Society of America, Inc.), General Council, Maryknoll, New York, U.S.A.

Evangelicals

Thomas Gutierrez, Executive Secretary, CEHILA, Lima, Peru

Aaron Gallegos, Sojourners Magazine, Washington, D.C., U.S.A.

REPRESENTATIVES FROM AREAS OF MISSION IN LATIN AMERICA AND THE CARIBBEAN

Daniel Vaccaro (Pentecostal), "Chicos de la Calle" (Street Children) Association, Buenos Aires, Argentina

Hector Peil (Work with Indigenous People), United Board of Missions (JUM), Prov. De Chaco, Argentina

Pablo Vieira (Youth-Urban Community), "Obra Ecuménica Barrio Borro," Evangelical Federation of Churches of Uruguay

Mara Vidal (African American Culture), NETMAL, São Paulo, Brazil

Ines P. de Sarli (Medical Doctor), Misión de Amistad, Asunción, Paraguay

Ivan Forero (Base Communities), Assembly of the People of God (APD), Santafe de Bogotá, Colombia

Ernestina Ochoa (Community Leader), IPROFOTH, Lima , Peru

Pilar Avendaño (Community Leader), Church World Service, Santiago, Chile

Timoteo Lima Quecana (Indian Community), CDR, Potosí, Bolivia

Antonio Estevez (Rural Community), Social Service of Dominican Churches, Santo Domingo, Dominican Republic

Polycarpe Joseph (Human Rights), Ecumenical Committee for Peace and Justice (COPJ), Fort Lauderdale, Florida, U.S.A.

Alfredo Ruiz (Human Rights), Support Network for Justice, Caracas, Venezuela

Natan Pravia (Indian Leader), Christian Commission for Development, Tegucigalpa, Honduras

Ofelia Alvarez Coleman (Indian Leader), CIEETS, Managua, Nicaragua

Gustavo Andrade (Human Rights), Diocese-San Cristobal de Las Casas, Chiapas, Mexico

Otilia Silva Leite (Work with Prostitutes), DAVIDA, Rio de Janeiro, Brazil

Vitalino Similox (Indigenous Leader), Evangelical Conference of Churches of Guatemala

Pablo Odén Marichal (Socialist Society), Cuban Council of Churches

Lázaro González (Socialist Society), Cuban Council of Churches

SPEAKERS

Walter Altmann, President, Latin American Council of Churches, São Leopoldo, Brazil

Joan Brown Campbell, General Secretary, National Council of the Churches of Christ in the USA, New York, New York, U.S.A.

Harvey Cox, Harvard University Divinity School, Cambridge, Massachusetts, U.S.A.

Zwinglio M. Dias, Advisor to the Missiology Consultation, *Koinonia*, Rio de Janeiro, Brazil

F. Ross Kinsler, Latin American Biblical Seminary, San José, Costa Rica

Luis Rivera-Pagán, Trujillo Alto, Puerto Rico

John Sinclair, Former Latin America Secretary, Presbyterian Church, USA Roseville, Minnesota , U.S.A.

Jung Mo Sung, São Paulo, Brazil

Elsa Tamez, Latin American Biblical Seminary, San José, Costa Rica

Jeremiah Wright, Trinity United Church of Christ, Chicago, Illinois, U.S.A.

LITURGY TEAM

Edwin Mora, Latin American Biblical Seminary, San José, Costa Rica

MOCRISCALEB (Musical Group), Cabudare, Estado Lara, Venezuela
   Eseario Sosa
   Herlinda C. Colmenares
   Edubert Ocanto Sanchez
   Uben Jara Jara

REGIONAL DELEGATES FROM COMMITTEES ON THE CARIBBEAN AND LATIN AMERICA

Noemi Espinoza, Mesoamerica, Christian Commission for Development, Tegucigalpa, Honduras (Evangelical Reformed)

Anastasio Gallego, Andean Region, Guayaquil, Ecuador (Roman Catholic)

Noemi Gorrin, CCLA Member-at-Large, Cuban Council of Churches (Pentecostal)

Guillermo Kerber, South Atlantic, Ecumenical Service for Human Dignity, Montevideo, Uruguay (Roman Catholic)

Pierre Philippe, Caribbean, Interdenominational Group of Pastors (GPI), Santo Domingo, Dominican Republic (Reformed)

NATIONAL COUNCIL OF THE CHURCHES OF CHRIST IN THE USA

Rodney I. Page, Executive Director, Church World Service & Witness Unit, New York, New York, U.S.A.

R. Lawrence Turnipseed, Advisor to CWS&W for Missiological Matters, New York, New York, U.S.A.

Oscar Bolioli, Director of the Latin America and the Caribbean Office, New York, New York, U.S.A.

Eva Jensen, Director, Agricultural Missions, New York, New York, U.S.A.

Samuel Lobato, Regional Representative, Mesoamerica Region, Mexico

Jane Sullivan Davis, Regional Representative, Andean Region, Santiago, Chile

Juan Santana, Aquaculture Technician, Santo Domingo, Dominican Republic

Mariela Shaw, Program Specialist, New York, New York, U.S.A.

Ana Soto, Program Assistant, New York, New York, U.S.A.

Luz Velasquez, Administrative Assistant, New York, New York, U.S.A.

CONFERENCE TRANSLATORS AND INTERPRETERS

Nancy Boye, Latin American Biblical Seminary (SBL), San José, Costa Rica

David Bronkema, Fairfield, Connecticut, U.S.A.

Elizabeth Cook, Latin American Biblical Seminary (SBL), San José, Costa Rica

Cynthia Diez and team, CARDISO Translators, San José, Costa Rica

Richard Foulkes, Latin American Biblical Seminary (SBL), San José, Costa Rica

Gloria Kinsler, Latin American Biblical Seminary (SBL), San José, Costa Rica

William Nottingham, Indianapolis, Indiana , U.S.A.

Donald Reasoner, New York, New York, U.S.A.

Mariela Shaw, New York, New York, U.S.A.

PRESS

Anibal Sicardi, Agencia de Noticias Prensa Ecuménica, Buenos Aires, Argentina

Carol Fouke, Communication, National Council of the Churches of Christ in the USA, New York, New York, U.S.A.

Ana Aslan, Photographer, Woodside, New York, U.S.A.